HOW ONE MAN OVERCAME TOURETTE'S SYNDROME
TO BECOME AN ACCLAIMED PROFESSIONAL MAGICIAN, AND
HOW YOU, TOO, CAN LIVE YOUR BIGGEST, BOLDEST LIFE

D0003221

YOU CAN DO
THE IMPOSSIBLE,
TOO!

JASON MICHAELS

COPYRIGHT

ISBN: 0-9989290-0-X
ISBN-13: 978-0-9989290-0-2

Cover Photo: Kris D'Amico

Back Cover Photo: Adam Sain

LET'S CONNECT!

Thank you for picking up my book! I'm excited that you are about to take this journey with me. I would love to keep in touch with you. The best way is through my monthly e-newsletter. I keep my friends up to date with the latest news, shows, speaking engagements, book signings, and more. That way we can meet in person someday! To sign up for my email list, visit my website...

www.JasonMichaelsMagic.com

We can also keep in touch on Social Media!

Twitter.com/jmichaelsmagic

Facebook.com/jmmagic

Instagram.com/jasonmichaelsisthecardshark

YouTube.com/JasonMichaelsMagic

DEDICATION

This book is dedicated to my family. My mom, dad, brother, and sister have always been my champions. I couldn't have been raised in a more loving, caring family. I had the best medical care we could find, even when we didn't have a clue what my problems were. I am emotionally healthy and my sense of self is strong today because of how nurturing and supportive my family was as I struggled to overcome the challenges that sometimes felt impossible. This is for Mike, Cindy, Brian, and Kristin.

Acknowledgments

If you had told me ten years ago that I would write a book that went into great detail about my struggles with Tourette's Syndrome and how I overcame "impossible" challenges, I would have told you it would never happen. The only reason I decided to start sharing my story with groups, and now with a book, is because of close friends who knew the challenges I deal with on a daily basis and never stopped pushing me to share them with the world.

First and foremost, thank you to The Lord. I have sometimes wondered why I was given such a difficult cross to bear. The truth is I wouldn't be the person I am today without all the challenges. Knowing that You always have my back gives me incredible strength and the endurance to run the entire race. You blessed me with an incredible family who took care of my every need. You also graced my path with amazing friends who have helped me see the value of sharing my story. You helped me identify my talents and gifts so I could share them with others. Now I ask that You take this book and use it to bless someone else's life the way You have blessed mine.

Thank you, Stephen Bargatze. You don't let up when you believe in someone. Thank you for helping me get more comfortable talking about a subject that I was very uncomfortable talking about for a long, long time.

Thank you, Kevin Propst. You helped me gain clarity as I worked toward becoming a full-time speaker. I appreciate how you nudged me in the right direction when I needed it.

Thank you, Nelson Griswold. You helped me see how "impossible" what I accomplished really was. You also knew what to say to keep the vision of a book in the back of my mind.

Thank you, Brett Daniels. I truly appreciate your friendship and mentorship. I learned important lessons working for you that shaped my life.

Thank you to Scott Cantrell, Bart Camarata, Corey West, Aarron Szalacinski, and John Pyka. I appreciate all your friendships.

Thank you to Dr. Barbara Olson and Dr. Michael Cooper who treated me for Tourette's Syndrome.

CONTENTS

INTRODUCTION

A S FAR BACK as I can remember, I have held certain societal norms in contempt. I've never really understood why a group of people in positions of power could make a set of rules that other people were then expected to follow.

I've never understood why another group of people would willingly subject themselves to certain behaviors and actions just so they would fit in with everyone else. Without trying to be overly offensive, it seems to me as if there are far too many sheep in the world who aren't willing to stand up against ridiculous rules, societal norms, and people who want to control everyone else.

Of course, given the tics and twitches of Tourette's Syndrome that make it all but impossible for me to easily blend into the crowd, it may be understandable that I have a deep disdain when it comes to rules and norms that don't seem to serve a purpose, other than to make my life more difficult.

Let me share an example with you. I was recently at a networking meeting with a group of business people. The speaker that day was talking about personal fashion and clothing choices for professionals.

The speaker reached a certain point in her presentation where she pointed out certain clothing choices that didn't fit in at business functions. She then decided to point out the fact that I was wearing a "t-shirt" at a networking event and how it was inappropriate.

I stood in shock as everyone in the room looked at me, the offending party. After the presentation was over, several people even had the gall to come up and poke fun at me for wearing something the speaker deemed "inappropriate."

I was furious. I even seriously considered putting the speaker "in her place." I opted for grace, decided against it, and kept my mouth shut. Little did the speaker, or anyone else in the room, know why I was wearing a shirt without a collar with a pair of slacks. Just for the record, the shirt I was wearing was not a "t-shirt." It was an appropriate, golf-style, uncollared shirt.

The reason I wasn't wearing "business attire" to the event is the same reason that my wardrobe is full of nice shirts without collars. It's because, when I wear a shirt, a tie, or anything that touches my neck, the tics of my Tourette's Syndrome fire off like crazy.

I know it sounds bizarre, but having anything touching my neck makes me twitch severely and uncontrollably. My "neck tics" get so out of control that I am unable to concentrate on anything, become exhausted quickly, and am extremely uncomfortable.

On the rare occasions when I do wear a collared shirt, tie, or suit for a formal occasion, I can't shed that clothing fast enough when the event is over. I've even been known to carry a bag of extra, comfortable clothing with me so I can change clothes in the bathroom at the event, as soon as possible.

The way I see it, when you have Tourette's Syndrome, and you get made fun of because of the weird movements or vocalizations that you unconsciously make, you can either pull back into your shell and feel like a victim when people bully and alienate you, or you can put on your armor, stand up against the negativity, and live boldly and fearlessly.

Adults make the rules for you as a child or teenager. Children are told what is appropriate and how they are expected to act. They tend to hear the word "no" a lot. No, you are too small to ride the roller coaster. No, you won't grow up to be a star football player. No, no, no.

As I reflect on my childhood, I understand that decisions were often made in my best interest. I wish I'd had the words to explain why being forced to wear a shirt, tie, and blazer to church or to a family picture felt like torture. All I knew was that I was expected to look and act a certain way, a way that society expected of me.

My experience taught me that trying to live up to society's standards and live by what is expected by others was a recipe for unhappiness. I have been as guilty as anyone of comparing myself to others and trying to live up to expectations that may have been unreasonable. The only thing living that way accomplished was to fill me with frustration and destructive self-talk.

Most of the time when you grow older, the adults around you stop telling you what to do or how to act. They may occasionally share their opinions with you, but other adults know they can't get away with telling you what you can and can't do. And while the adults used to tell you "no," now you have a much stiffer adversary telling you no. Yourself. You are the one who limits what you can and can't do.

One of my biggest personal barriers to overcome has been the quiet times, late in the evening, when I am full of doubt. I don't show any doubt and reservations when I am in public, but from time to time I wonder if I've made smart decisions in my life. It is at those times that I beat myself up with destructive self-talk.

The way we talk to ourselves is embarrassing. "No, you'll never be a success." "No, you'll never get out of debt." "No, you don't have enough talent or intelligence or drive, or whatever is necessary, to live your dreams." If we heard an adult speaking to a child this way, we would chastise the adult for such harsh language and for trying to kill the child's spirit.

We are constantly in a battle against negativity and the word "No." We battle outside forces, we battle other people, and we battle our most difficult adversary — ourselves.

I wish I knew why we are constantly bombarded with such negativity. I wish I knew why it appears that the world sometimes conspires against us, but I don't.

What I have learned over my lifetime is that we have a choice. We can choose to listen to the haters. We can choose to give in to self-doubt in moments of weakness. We can prove that all the critics were right about us.

Or, we can fight back. We can say yes to those who tell us no. We can take the beating that life sometimes dishes out, and get up off the mat swinging. We can identify and surround ourselves with people who believe in us and who champion us on to the greatness that is within.

We can listen to the still, small voice deep inside of us that helps us identify our dreams and keeps us on the right course. We can choose to believe in ourselves, imagine ourselves conquering every obstacle, and take actions that accomplish those goals. We can live big, exciting lives.

My choice is to don my armor, get in the ring, and fight. And if you have picked up this book, then I believe you also have chosen to fight. So, let's fight together.

This is my story of fighting back against everyone and everything that has tried to keep me from living the life that I was created to live. This is my story of saying yes to those who said no. This is my story of overcoming the odds, massive self-doubt, and other people who said I could never do the things I wanted to do in my life. This is my story of doing the impossible.

The simple truth is that I never wanted to write this story. For decades, I viewed my Tourette's Syndrome as "a weakness" that was embarrassing, alienating, and set me apart from everyone and labeled me as "weird." Only when a close friend several years ago set an amazing example for me did I understand why it was important for me to open up and share my experiences.

If you are suffering from Tourette's Syndrome, I put all of this down on paper so that you would know that you aren't alone. Being the only person in the room twitching, tic-ing, and making weird noises can make you feel like you are very alone. And when other people look at you while laughing and making snide comments, it can be quite painful.

When the uncontrollable movements go on and on and on, I know that it feels like your own personal Hell, one that will never end. And yes, it is absolutely torturous in the moment to think that it is possible that you will be dealing with these tics for the rest of your life.

My prayer for you is that you will read my story and see that there is life beyond the tics. Sometimes your Tourette's will beat you up badly and it will be hard to see past your immediate, painful situation. Do not give up and do not give in. You have incredible gifts and blessings to share with the rest of us.

It may be almost impossible for you to see right now, but you have and will continue to develop an incredible perspective on the world because of your T.S. Some of the gifts that I have developed are empathy, drive, appreciating life in the moment, standing up against bullies, and an iron will to succeed.

As a teenager with this disorder, I certainly didn't understand that I would grow up to live the life of my dreams and have some incredible adventures. I sincerely hope that you and I meet one day in the future and you will tell me about some of your own adventures.

If you have a family member or friend with Tourette's Syndrome and you decided to read this book in the hope that you would gain some insight into how to treat your loved one, how to care for your loved one, or how to understand what your loved one is going through, I have some advice. These are the qualities that will serve you well – patience, love, and understanding (as best you can).

As a young person with Tourette's Syndrome, I often wondered why I had it. It didn't seem fair that I had it. No one else I knew had T.S. Was I cursed? Had I done something wrong and this was my punishment? Why did I have to go through all the frustration and difficulty with the tics and no one else did?

Even when I was officially diagnosed with Tourette's and could put a name to the weird movements and vocalizations, it still didn't seem fair. And you know what? It wasn't fair, but it was life. As we all know, life isn't always fair.

I'm reminded of the saying, "Don't miss the forest for the trees." Your loved one with Tourette's often may focus on the trees – the day-to-day difficulties that T.S. brings. Sometimes it will be very difficult for them to see the forest – the big picture of life.

Your patience on the days when the tics are unbearable, your understanding that your loved one is dealing with very difficult circumstances, and your unconditional love for them will be the rock that they will stand on.

When everything seems to be falling apart in your loved one's life, knowing that you care and that you support him or her will give them a much-needed sense of stability. They may not be able to control themselves at all times, but knowing that you are standing firmly in their corner will give them a sense of control.

If you just happened to check out this book because you are interested in the art of magic, you will get a unique look at what it is like to pursue magic and entertainment as a career. I think you'll find the stories and adventures interesting. They were almost as much fun to write about as they were to live.

The magic community is tightly knit. I've met most of my closest friends because of our shared love of magic, sleight-of-hand, and illusion. We keep our secrets close to our vests, but we also welcome newcomers who genuinely want to learn. If, after you've read my story, you want to dive deeper into magic, let me be the first to welcome you to an incredible hobby, part-time job, or career.

If you just happened to check this book out because it looked interesting, thank you! I hope you'll dive in and spend some visiting with me. On these pages are a story of a life lived boldly.

I firmly believe that we are all on this planet together so we can help each other navigate our way through life. The simple truth is that we all deal with limitations. It's how we respond to those limitations and circumstances that define who we become and where we go in life.

I would be humbled and honored if reading my story gave you the inspiration and motivation to start taking the steps to overcome any limitations or circumstances that feel "impossible" in your life.

CHAPTER ONE

D@MN! SH!T! H*LL! D@mn! @ss! Sh!t!

I figured we should get the cursing out of the way early. That is what you think Tourette's Syndrome is, right? Well, that's what a great many people know about the disorder. They think it's the weird neurological disorder that makes you curse. And for a small percentage of people with the syndrome, that is exactly what it is. But for the vast majority of us with it, Tourette's Syndrome isn't nearly so interesting.

Let me tell you a story…

I sat in the passenger's seat one morning, next to my Dad, on my way to school. I think I was six years old. As we made our way across town I was rubbing my chin against my collarbone. I kept doing it over and over and I couldn't stop. I was starting to grow frustrated because I just kept doing this movement and I was completely out of control of my own body. And as much as I wanted to stop, my body just wouldn't. I had been doing this movement on and off for several days and my neck was starting to get red and raw.

This is the first memory I have of experiencing one of the "tics" of Tourette's Syndrome. Interestingly, I remember this instance decades later because of the frustration I felt from not being able to control myself. And if you've never had an experience where your body starts doing an action that you are not in control of, it can be hard to understand how such a thing is possible.

One moment everything in your world is completely normal; the next moment you are shaking your head over and over, or making strange clicking noises with your tongue, or reading the same passage in a book over and over, unable to move your eyes to the next line. I think that is what is so difficult for teachers and other adults to understand about the children who deal with the involuntary tics of Tourette's Syndrome.

What makes Tourette's Syndrome feel so "impossible" to someone who lives with it is the helplessness. I like to think that I'm a fairly intelligent person. I reason well. I am also very intuitive around others. But for all my "intelligence," my ability to reason, and my social awareness, I simply couldn't stop shaking, twitching, or making strange vocalizations.

The reason I felt so helpless was because of my ability to reason and think. Most of life is cause and effect. When you take an action, there is a reaction. That is what we learn about the world around us.

What is not understandable as a young child (and sometimes is difficult to understand as an adult), is why you are making these distracting, sometimes very uncomfortable movements.

It feels like you are only seeing effect – the movements, with no cause to attribute them to.

My mom tells me that she knew something was "off" with me all the way back in my infancy. She could see small signs that only a mother, or someone who was very in tune with a baby, could see. And while she didn't have any idea what was going on at that time, she told me that she knew something abnormal was going on.

Even though I was dealing with an unknown disorder, my childhood was fantastic. I was so incredibly fortunate and blessed to be born into a family who provided for all my needs, did everything possible to help me grow mentally, physically, and spiritually, and was there every single day with kind words and support.

I was around seven years old when my mom and dad took me to see a psychologist. I remember being in this nice man's office and feeling like I was being watched. I've always been aware when I have been in situations, like doctor's offices, where people were observing me.

I wish I could have been more relaxed and allowed the tics to display themselves freely, but I have never felt comfortable putting my "weakness" on display.

So, instead of allowing the tics to manifest, I did two things. First, I could suppress the tics a little bit because of the hyper-focus I had during that office visit. The second thing I did was to "mask" the tics that I was displaying in everyday movements. Let me explain…

I know that you are probably wondering what the heck I'm talking about. After all, I just told you a few minutes ago that the tics of T.S. aren't controllable. And generally speaking, that's true.

My "normal" Tourette's Syndrome tics occur without warning. One minute I might be busy doing something like typing on the computer keyboard; the next minute my arm is flailing around over my head without warning.

However, what I have learned is that when I am in specific, pressure-filled situations where I know that I am being watched, or where it is very inappropriate to call attention to myself, I can focus my attention so that the tics are suppressed for a brief period. I call this "hyper-focus."

I think I can suppress the tics because, ultimately, I am trying to blend in with the crowd or the situation. In other words, I don't want to draw unwanted attention to myself, which would put me in an embarrassing situation where I might have to explain my T.S. to someone I don't know.

For me, the idea that I might be ostracized or made fun of for something that I, ultimately, have no control over is such a deterrent that I am able to focus my attention so that my only goal is to not have a twitch, tic, or vocalization. And that hyper-focus works, for a short period of time.

As a child, I made friends easily and I don't remember getting made fun of on a frequent basis. When someone did say something hurtful, which happened from time to time, it made a deep impact on me.

I remember being in the church van on my way to kids' choir practice after grade school one day. I was sitting with several of my friends in the back of the van when the prettiest girl I knew made a joke about my twitching. All my friends laughed at me while I sat there embarrassed about something I had no control over.

There I sat, everyone surrounding me on the van, looking at me and laughing at me. I was in the spotlight, but not for a good reason. To add insult to injury, the one girl who I secretly liked and was hoping liked me, was the one making fun of me. That hurt.

It didn't take many situations like that one before I taught myself how to "hyper focus" and mask my tics when I knew that people were watching me.

Another example of my hyper-focus came when I was a teenager taking a Karate class that I absolutely loved. Karate is a very physical martial art and I excelled at it. In Karate class, there were times when all the students stood "at attention" in a straight line. When you were standing "at attention," you were expected to stand still and pay attention to what the teacher was talking about or demonstrating. Those times, standing "at attention," took a great deal of effort for me.

As my skill level progressed, so did the amount of effort that the advanced Karate classes required. By the end of a class, I might be completely exhausted. And while that is wonderful exercise and great for discipline — being hyper focused — it came with a level of physical exhaustion that was a perfect recipe for an unbelievable amount of violent tics and twitches as soon as I was able to let down physically and relax my mental focus.

In addition to my hyper-focus helping me suppress my tics, I am positive that it also aided my learning of Karate. I paid very close attention in class and I learned quickly. My ability to focus on the techniques combined with good coordination helped me excel in class.

There would be nights after Karate class when I would lay on the floor in front of the television and shake my head over and over again, so violently that I almost threw my neck out.

I've often thought, when I left a place where I had to be hyper-focused and I started to twitch and tic, that it was time for me to "pay the piper." I knew that I could "control" the tics in most situations just long enough to not be noticed by others. But after I left those situations, the tics and twitches were going to "get caught up" and I was going to have a difficult period full of sudden, rapid, repetitive, uncontrollable movements.

By the way, these terms are terms that I have made up based on what it felt like I was doing at the time. I'm not using any medical terms that I'm aware of to describe what I felt.

Now you might be wondering what I meant when I mentioned that I could "mask" the tics. Because it has always been very important to me to not be singled out or be made fun of in social settings, I unconsciously developed a technique that I would use when I knew someone was watching me and trying to detect any strange movements. I call it "masking."

To "mask" a tic would be to incorporate that movement into a larger movement that appeared to be a normal looking movement. It is much akin to the sleight-of-hand techniques that magicians use when they perform magic tricks. When explaining why some sleight-of-hand techniques work, a veteran magician will instruct an up-and-coming magician that a small movement can be covered by a larger movement.

In other words, if a magician is executing a sleight-of-hand technique that may happen at his fingertips, he or she might turn his or her entire body at the exact same time. A spectator may believe the magician turned his or her body so that it would be easier for the spectator to see what the magician was doing. The actual reason, though, is because the larger action of turning his entire body makes the smaller action of the technique at his fingertips completely invisible.

That is exactly what I do when I "mask" the tics. What is hard to explain is that the "masking" technique is almost done unconsciously. I can't emphasize enough how much I try to blend in during my everyday life. Being noticed by others, being laughed at, or being questioned by a stranger about what kind of weird movement I was just doing has always been a deeply painful and embarrassing position for me.

Let me give you another example. Sometimes I rapidly twitch my head to the side a few inches. If I do that, then notice that someone has started watching me, I will "mask" it.

If the twitch happens again, I will pretend to be looking at something specific in the direction of where I just moved my head. I may even comment about something that I'm looking at.

Other times I will rub my neck with one of my hands, immediately after the tic happens, while muttering under my breath that I have a crick in my neck. By "masking" the twitch, I am able to camouflage the tic with a normal looking movement that most normal people will discount. Then the person watching me will go back to doing whatever it was they were doing before they noticed my tics.

Of course, when I was a kid, I had no idea I was developing a technique to camouflage my tics that magicians used in their performances. That realization would come much later.

I was twelve years old when we were finally able to "officially" give a name to the strange movements that I had been making my entire life. I had what was called Tourette's Syndrome, and I learned that it was a neurological disorder – a brain disorder – that was still being studied and learned about.

It was a good thing to be able to identify and attach a name to the malady I was dealing with. It was good to know that the medical community knew what it was and was actively trying to treat it.

But there were no effective treatments. Oh, there were treatments that worked for some people, but which might not work for other people. Or the treatments might be somewhat effective, but the side effects of the drugs were as bad, or worse, than the tics.

I took drugs with names like Klonopin, Haldol, and Prozac. In fact, because many of these drugs were prescribed for people with other mental issues, I remember having talks with my parents about feeling, or being labeled, "crazy."

I didn't feel "crazy." But these were drugs that were taken by people with depression, seizures, schizophrenia, panic disorder, and all sorts of other fun stuff. And you definitely start to wonder about yourself when the drug you are taking is an antipsychotic.

I guess the truth is that "crazy" people have no idea that they are "crazy," because they are living that reality. I mean if you are deep in the trees, how can you see the forest? But I could see the forest.

I had been living with these uncontrollable physical movements and vocal noises for years. And while I couldn't control them, I could see them for what they were — physical actions caused by a chemical imbalance in my brain. That chemical imbalance did not extend beyond the movements and vocalizations into my reasoning and emotional abilities.

One of the most interesting parts of having Tourette's Syndrome is that there are times in my life when I may have very heavy periods of tics and twitches, and there are other times when the tics and twitches virtually vanish. The medical community calls it waxing and waning.

During a waxing period, the tics would be especially strong. I might deal with one specific tic, like head twitching, or I might deal with multiple tics at the same time, like head twitching, making clicking noises with my tongue, and flailing my left arm around repeatedly. These were the times when I felt like I was going through my own personal version of Hell.

Waxing periods can last for different lengths of time. I have noticed that my tics get much more pronounced when my body has been stressed in some way.

My mom was the first person to point out to me that immediately after I have been sick, my tics were much more severe. The best way to explain what happens is like this...I get sick and my body must use all its energy to get better; then I get over the sickness and feel better, and then the tics hit in full force.

In a way, it is similar to the way I described what would happen at Karate class. I (or my body) would be so focused on the task at hand (trying to get well from my sickness) that I (or my body) would have a hyper-focus (on getting well). Then, after the task was complete (and I got over the sickness) and my Tourette's Syndrome wasn't suppressed by the hyper-focus anymore, the tics returned with intensity and it was time for me to "pay the piper."

Other instances when my tics are more severe is when I don't get enough sleep and my body is run down and worn out. Basically, if something happens to my body to throw it out of balance, I can directly attribute that to the tics that show up heavily when my body gets back to normal.

I have several theories of why the tics wax stronger during certain times of my life. Some of those theories include when my allergies are heavy or when I eat certain foods. My mom believes that the Strep virus triggers heavy periods of tics.

How long does a waxing period last? It's hard to say. For me it could last for days, weeks, even months. There was a time in my twenties and early thirties when I stopped taking all sorts of medications and the tics, more or less, pretty much went away. However, as I got into my mid-thirties, they returned and I was forced to seek medical treatment again.

Currently, the heaviest periods of tics do not last more than a few days. But I would be lying to you if I didn't tell you when I was younger there were times when I had very pronounced tics that lasted for months, and sometimes longer.

It is during those periods of heavy tics when I must be very aware of the way I talk to myself. In my normal life, I am extremely upbeat and positive. I am excited every day to see what's going to happen. However, when I deal with day-in and day-out of heavy tics, I get easily exhausted and frustrated.

During those times of frustration and exhaustion, I sometimes catch myself focusing on the negative aspects of my life. Instead of feeling like a conqueror and a champion, I feel like a victim. I blame the Tourette's Syndrome for the things in my life that I am dissatisfied with.

When I was a kid, I would think about all the drugs I was taking and think about how I was just a step away from being "crazy." As an adult, I tend to focus on whatever I happen to be unhappy with at that moment. Most of the time, I end up complaining to myself that I am not successful enough in my business.

Over time, I have learned that this defeating self-talk is not based in reality. It only appears when I am extremely tired, and most of the time that happens because of an extreme case of tics.

I deal with it by identifying how I feel and realizing that it is a temporary situation. I also have learned that most of the defeating self-talk occurs late in the day, when I am exhausted. I know that a good night's sleep will often do wonders for my mental state.

The good news for me is that there is also a waning period of time that comes with the tics. I never really appreciate the waning periods until the tics start back up again. Then I realize how nice it was to have enjoyed an interim (sometimes a long period of time) with no extraneous movements or undue attention focused on me.

Did the medications and treatments work? The jury's out on that one. I think that sometimes the drugs did help. But because they only diminished the tics a small amount, it felt to me like they weren't working at all. The most frustrating part for me as a young person was that the treatment included me having to cycle on and off different drugs while we tried to find something that actually helped.

I would begin a new medication and start by taking an introductory level dose. Then we (mostly my parents) would monitor my tics and track the medication's effect on them. Then we would up the medication to a higher dose to see if that diminished the tics even more. The process could take months or years to assess whether one specific medication helped. To be honest, it was sort of infuriating.

Think about it this way. When you are violently twitching over and over again, minute after minute, hour after hour, over days and weeks, and even months, it seems absolutely asinine to take months or years just to figure out if your medication actually worked! But that was my reality.

And drug-testing took longer sometimes because you honestly couldn't tell if the drug was helping suppress the tics, or if I just happened to be in one of the waning states that came with the disorder.

I remember one time my doctor asking me if I thought a drug I was taking was helping. I honestly had no clue. I really couldn't tell. It felt like the entire treatment process of my childhood and youth was like this. And for me, that was very frustrating and difficult.

As I was dealing with figuring out medications and treatments, I still had normal life to tend to. And what was very obvious to me was that sometimes real-life isn't very kind. And while real life can be painful, my mother was going to make damn sure that my life was the best it could possibly be.

Because when you sometimes twitch and tic and unknowingly grab other people's attention, you become very aware of the hurtful and mean things that some people say to you. Even if those people choose not to say the mean things, you know it is always a very real possibility that they might say them.

I recall standing in the grocery store one day in the cereal aisle. Because I was busy looking at the different cereals trying to find something that looked tasty, I didn't see the lady walking up the aisle. As I reached onto the shelf to pick out my cereal selection, this complete stranger started laughing out loud at me as she said, "Whoa! Everything okay there, buddy?"

I immediately turned her way and said, "Oh yeah, I've just got a crick in my neck."

That response is yet another way that I would "mask" my tics. In addition to "masking" them through other movements, I also had a couple of normal sounding explanations for the strange-looking movements I made.

That situation in the grocery store really wasn't a big deal. The lady didn't make fun of me. She did, however, laugh at me. For some reason, this one instance stuck in my mind for years, perhaps because I was taken so off-guard. I thought the medications were helping with my tics and this situation just proved that, no matter how hard we tried to treat the twitching, it just wouldn't go away completely.

Both my mom and my dad were my champions. My mom, however, went to war for me against anyone and everyone who might say something hurtful. And she made sure that my teachers knew who I was, what I was dealing with, and how to best work with me.

I have a vague memory of being a young person and having a discussion with my mom one day about whether I wanted her to talk to my teachers about my Tourette's. Later in life, I found out that she had been having these discussions with my teachers for years, but this time she included me in the conversation.

I remember being a little torn about having to tell someone else that I had this weird disorder, but ultimately, I remember being relieved that someone knew and would (sort of) understand. My hope, by having my mom tell my teachers, was that they would be champions for me the same way that my parents were.

I really didn't want any special treatment. All I wanted was to be treated like everything was normal. I've never wanted to be singled out. I've never wanted to be given preferential treatment over anyone else. I've never wanted anyone to look at me as I twitched and ask if I was okay. All I've ever wanted was to just be like everyone else going about my life. "Excuse me, sir. Please ignore the weird movements and noises, and just let me be like everybody else."

And for most of my childhood and teenage years I was. I was just like everyone else. I blended in. I had my friends. I was treated pretty normally. But everything changed when I was sixteen years old.

CHAPTER TWO

WE ALL HAVE defining moments in life. I was fortunate because several of my defining moments came when I was sixteen years old, a relatively young age. At the time I didn't know they were defining moments, but I did know that these moments were energizing, exciting, and opened up my life, my mind, and my imagination to new possibilities.

I enrolled in Speech and Drama class my junior year of high school. I had taken two years of art class and, technically, didn't need any more liberal arts (electives) classes like that to graduate. But it sounded like fun and I wanted to give it a try.

My speech and drama class was focused on two different things – speech, or forensics, which was basically a dramatic or humorous interpretation of a story shared by a student tasked with finding powerful moments in literature and recreating them for an audience; and drama, or doing scene work and theatrical plays.

If I'm being honest, I didn't feel like my strength fell in the forensics side of things. I just didn't relate to dramatically reading a story to a panel of judges and being judged on it. I wasn't bad at it, I just didn't feel like it was my thing. It didn't feel real to me. Drama, however, was a completely different beast.

One day I was sitting in class looking over some short scenes on a piece of photocopied paper when my teacher announced that in several days she was holding auditions for the Junior/Senior play.

In my school, when you were a junior or a senior, you were eligible to audition. This was the big play for the fall semester. This was a big deal, the play that everyone came to see.

I had never auditioned for a play. Heck, I had barely even spent any time on a stage. But the Junior/Senior play sounded like fun. So, I decided to audition.

Let's stop and think about that for a second. Here I was, a sixteen-year-old guy with a neurological disorder that manifested itself with uncontrollable movements and vocal tics, deciding to audition for a play that most of the school would come to see. Does this sound like a recipe for disaster to you? Because looking back, it doesn't seem like a course of action that I would advise a young person to take.

Up until this point of my life, all I wanted was to not be noticed and embarrassed or be alienated. Now I was actively seeking out the spotlight. What kind of madness was this?

This was definitely a bad idea. After all, if I didn't make a fool of myself during auditions and somehow managed to get a part in the play, I would be expected to say the right lines at the right times during the play itself. And that was a big "if."

There was a big chance that I would walk up onstage during auditions and not be able to say the right lines at the right times. There was also a big chance that instead of saying the words that my character was supposed to say, that I would, instead, have a vocal tic or start twitching uncontrollably.

Let's consider the best-case scenario for a minute. Let's just accept the unlikely, but hopeful idea that I might get through auditions and get a role in the play. If that actually happened, I would be a part of a team of actors trying to successfully stage the most important production of the year in front of our entire school.

And what if I made it all the way through auditions and rehearsals and then, when an audience was present, the tics started up. Because, when the white-hot spotlight hits you and it's your turn to say your lines, you can't sink back into the shadows.

Oh…my…gosh! If that actually happened, all the years that I spent trying to not be noticed and not be made fun of would be over. I would be the guy who choked onstage. I would be the guy who "twitched" at my school. Everybody in my entire school would have something to say directly to me and plenty more to say about me behind my back. I would constantly be made fun of for the rest of my school life.

One of my recurring tics over my lifetime is when I rub my chin against my neck and collarbone. I can't count how many times I've almost slammed right into people because I was walking around a corner while doing this tic. It was embarrassing enough in high school for one of the football players to yell, "Hey, watch out man!" Did I really want to risk auditioning for the school play, and maybe getting a part?

Getting a part in the Junior/Senior play was impossible for a guy like me. It sounded fun, but in reality, it was a terrible idea. It was fun to dream about what it might be like performing a great show in front of an adoring audience, but that wasn't my reality.

My reality was that I was destined to twitch and tic in strange, embarrassing ways my entire life. The smart thing for me to do was to realize that certain things in my life just weren't possible, and that I should go on living my life in ways that would keep all the attention off me.

Fortunately, I've never been accused of always choosing to do the safe, "smart" things in life. And besides, I had a healthy disdain for the rules and norms of society by this point in my life.

On reflection, I don't remember thinking about auditioning for the play like that at all. My teacher made the announcement, it sounded like fun, I had admired the performers group that I had seen during my freshman and sophomore years, and I wanted to give it a try. After all, what would my life be like if I became one of the "famous" kids at my school?

Instead of wondering about all the bad things that could possibly happen if I got cast in the play, I fantasized about what would happen if I auditioned, got a part, and became one of the popular people. Maybe everyone would be staring at me for all the right reasons; they would be applauding and laughing because I was a star. Instead of being the kid who made the weird movements, I would in the public eye on my own terms, because I wanted to be.

The fact that I had Tourette's Syndrome and that, maybe, drawing attention to myself wasn't such a good idea, didn't enter my mind at all.

I showed up the first day of auditions and had no idea what was going to take place. I was given a sheet of paper that had been photocopied from the script and was told that I would be reading one of the character's monologues. The monologue was a paragraph or two and my job was to make the words on the page come alive.

Hmmm…a dramatic reading. Hmmm…this seemed a lot like forensics. The big difference was that at this dramatic reading there was an audience. There were people who would be actively listening and reacting to what I was saying and doing. There was a goal in sight – get a part in the play. Those two things made a difference. So, I stood on stage and read.

Next, everyone took part in scene work. I was paired with other actors and given another few photocopied pages of the script. We were reading the lines of the character we were assigned to read and then reacting to the lines that the other actors were delivering. This actually felt like acting to me. And it felt good. It felt natural.

When the audition came to an end we were told that the following morning on the theatre's bulletin board, right outside of the front door of the theatre, a callback sheet would be posted. A callback is what happens when an actor is asked to come back and continue the audition process while being considered with a smaller group of other actors. Basically, if you don't make the callback list, you're not getting a part.

That night I was nervous. All I could think about was making callbacks. I even dreamt of seeing my name on the piece of paper posted on the bulletin board.

To say that I was nervous as I approached the bulletin board the next morning might be an understatement. I really, really, really wanted my name to be on the list. I had seen it in my mind and I wanted to see it with my eyes, too. I had actively tried not to think about how disappointed I would be if I didn't make the cut.

As I walked up to the bulletin board, a piece of paper was posted. It was the callback list. I could immediately tell that the number of names on the list was a lot smaller than the number of people who had been at last night's audition. I scanned the list and saw the names of lots of seniors. And then I saw it. Two-thirds of the way down the list I saw my name. I had made it past the first cut. I had made callbacks. I had a chance at actually getting a role in the Junior/Senior play!

That night at callbacks I did more of the same things I did the first night. I read more monologues and did more scene work with different actors. I thoroughly enjoyed reading different characters' lines and getting to practice different scenes with the other actors. I was having a blast! The entire process was exhilarating!

At the end of the callback auditions, my teacher, who was also the director of the play, told us that she would post the list of the actors who had made the cast, and what role they were going to be playing, on the theatre bulletin board first thing in the morning.

I felt good about the whole process. Perhaps the most interesting thing that happened during the auditions was based on the amount of time that I had onstage. Up until then, I hadn't had a lot of time onstage. During the audition process though, I had a lot of time onstage. And I felt good there. It wasn't nerve-racking. It wasn't scary. I just felt comfortable. I felt peaceful on the stage in the theatre space. I felt like I was at home.

That night, I again dreamt of what it would be like to get a role in the play. And while I was a little nervous, I also knew that I had a really good shot at getting something. After all, why would I be given the chance to read multiple monologues and do the amount of scene work that I did during the audition?

The next day when I arrived at the theatre bulletin board I was flabbergasted. I honestly couldn't believe what I saw. I would have been thrilled to have gotten any role. I knew that most of the juicy roles would be given to seniors. After all, they had the experience and had put in the time. They were the ones who deserved them. I just wanted a part, any part in the play.

What I saw was my name at the top of the cast list and, across from my name, the name of the lead character in the play. I looked again to make sure that I was seeing it correctly. Had I gotten the lead role? Here I was, a junior in high school, with virtually no formal theatre training or experience, and I had just been cast in the lead role in my school's most prestigious play!

Words do not adequately describe the level of excitement and amazement that I experienced when I finally was able to process what had happened.

What had happened was this…when I was onstage focused on delivering a monologue or taking part in a scene with several other actors, I was focused on what I was doing. What I wasn't doing was twitching. I wasn't having any sort of vocal tics. The level of hyper-focus that I explained earlier took over and wouldn't allow the Tourette's to manifest while I was acting.

On reflection, maybe this outcome should have been predictable. After all, I had always been very sensitive to being embarrassed or alienated by anyone. Why wouldn't I be able to control a disorder that was uncontrollable long enough to perform in a play?

And perform in a play I did. Participating in that show started a love affair with live performance and with theatre that has lived inside of me ever since. I loved the rehearsal process. The familial atmosphere that is created when a group of actors works together in the pressure cooker that is a live show amazed me. I created my own techniques for memorizing page after page of lines for my character. And when opening night of the play "Don't Tell Mother!" arrived, I was ready.

On opening night, I didn't know how I was supposed to feel. I had heard that walking out in front of a large audience was terrifying. I had heard that stage fright is even normal for seasoned actors. I was excited, no doubt. But I didn't really have any feelings of what I thought stage fright was supposed to feel like.

I had worked very hard to learn my lines. I knew them cold. You could pick out any part of the script and feed me the line before mine and I could pick up right there and deliver my next line. I had worked hard in rehearsal. I knew where I was supposed to be onstage at every moment and I knew who and how to interact with the other actors onstage.

And then that inevitable moment came. The lights went down. The audience went silent. I took my place and the show began. When it was time, I entered the stage and I was off like a shot. Any self-doubt that I might have had vanished as I delivered my lines, interacted with the other actors, got laughs from the audience, and had the time of my life.

Here I am onstage at Gallatin High School's Junior/Senior play "Don't Tell Mother!"

I had a lot of raw talent and I was naturally good at the craft of acting. The question is why? Why did I deliver the lines well? Why did I have great rapport with the other actors? How could I share the right emotions with the audience at the right times? The answer is empathy.

Empathy is the ability to be able to identify and experience the thoughts, feelings, or attitudes of others. And I was very empathetic, for two reasons.

The first reason is because of my parents. As a child I remember my parents always asking me about how the things I was choosing to do in my life would impact other people and make them feel. And because I was posed this question many times, and I honestly thought about the question and cared about other people's feelings, I developed a sense for how other people were affected by my actions.

The other reason I was so empathetic was because of my own situation with Tourette's Syndrome. I don't recall any major issues of being bullied as a child, but that doesn't mean that hurtful things were never said, or that some people didn't try to make me feel small and worthless from time to time. Of course those things happened.

When you are empathetic and in touch with your emotions, it doesn't take many embarrassing instances to make an impact on you. You don't forget the moments when the girl that you like in school makes fun of your tics, or the high school football player tells you to "Watch out!" and people look at you funny.

Having my feelings hurt and being made fun of were painful experiences, but they helped me develop empathy. Those experiences helped me realize just how other people feel when hurtful things are said to them. Those experiences helped me tap into my feelings and my emotions. Ultimately, those experiences helped me become a naturally good actor.

What I did not expect when I walked onstage was the same feeling of peace to wash over me that I had felt in the past. Instead of terror or massive stage fright, there I was... out there on stage, standing in front of my peers, doing my thing. No tics. No twitches. No vocal noises.

And at the end of the show, I walked onstage for the last time that night to take my bow and the audience erupted. I had done it. I had done what should have been impossible for me to do. I had become an actor, and in the process found my life's calling... or so I thought.

CHAPTER THREE

I STOOD TRANSFIXED, STARING at all sorts of interesting gadgets sitting inside the glass cases just inches away. If it wasn't for the glass barrier, I could reach out and touch them. These gadgets were magic as far as I knew. And up on the shelves were all sorts of colorful tubes and boxes stenciled with oriental lettering. This place was like nowhere else I had ever been.

I had found my way into Abracadabra, the magic shop out by the airport in Nashville, TN, and I had no idea what any of this stuff was.

What brought me here? Let's back up a little.

I've been told that my grandfather used to do little magic tricks for me and the other grandkids when I was a child. I have no doubt that he did, but I just don't remember it. I've even been told that one of my great uncles and aunts even brought me a magic kit when they returned home from their travels when I was a kid. And as much as I hate to say it, I don't remember that either.

I wish I could turn to one of those instances as the moment in my life that I fell in love with magic. It just didn't happen like that for me. I have no doubt that both my grandfather and my aunt and uncle planted seeds that bloomed into an interest in magic. But I trace some very specific moments in my life that led me to that fateful day at the magic shop.

I don't recall the exact age, but I must have been somewhere between eight and twelve, when my grandmother taught me how to play solitaire. I'm sure that teaching me solitaire, a card game that you play by yourself, was an excellent way to keep an energetic and curious kid busy for an hour or two.

And while I don't remember the exact age I learned the game, I do have a wonderful memory of the learning experience. I sat next to my grandmother, who was playing a game of Solitaire, while she taught me how to play correctly.

Several years later, my grandfather introduced my dad, brother, cousins, uncle, and me to a game called Skip Bo. My family and I spent many Saturday afternoons over a period of years sitting in my grandparent's den playing Skip Bo with my grandfather.

When I was a junior in high school, several of my buddies and I started playing poker on Friday nights. In fact, we were having so much fun it quickly become a regular Friday night plan. We would all get together at my or one of my friend's houses and we would play poker in exchange for red, white, and blue plastic chips that each of us had purchased from "the bank" with a couple of dollars and a bunch of spare change.

Poker night when I was a junior in high school.

What a thrill those poker nights were. We were gambling (!) against each other, trying our best not to lose the couple of bucks we had invested. After all, if you lost several hands and ran out of chips you couldn't play anymore unless you bought more chips.

One day I started wondering how everyone would react if I did a card trick. I didn't know any card tricks and I couldn't recall ever having seen any card tricks. But for some reason, I thought it might be fun to try and 'wow' all my buddies with a card trick.

The only problem was that now I had to find a place where I could learn a card trick. My solution… the bookstore.

I had always enjoyed reading and the bookstore seemed a logical place to find out how to do card tricks. So, I made my way to the bookstore.

What is interesting is that I really didn't have any interest in learning any magic tricks. All I wanted to do was find a book that would teach me some easy-to-learn, really cool card tricks.

Fortunately for me, my theory was correct. The bookstore was the place to go to learn some cool card tricks. The store I visited had an entire section on magic, puzzles, chess, poker, and most importantly, card tricks.

After looking over a couple of different choices, I opted for a book titled "Scarne on Card Tricks". It was a small red book with a subtitle that read, "The Exact Details of 150 Professional Card Tricks – with no sleight-of-hand required. All Explained And Demonstrated By The One And Only John Scarne." Above the main title at the very top of the book it read, "You Will Be Amazed At How Easily You Can Amaze Others-With This Famous Book By The World's #1 Wizard With Cards."

That was right up my alley. I didn't know anything about sleight-of-hand, other than the fact that it was supposed to be very hard to learn. Obviously, sleight-of-hand wasn't something I would ever be able to do. But the idea that I could learn 150 professional card tricks, and that I would easily be able to amaze others, was something that I liked the sound of.

Reading a magic book, or in my case, a book on card tricks, is a thrill. The way that most authors write books on these subjects is to explain the "effect" first. That is, what the audience is going to experience, if the reader pulls off the trick successfully. And that is what is so thrilling.

You have to imagine me, with no experience performing card or magic tricks whatsoever, reading this book that has promised to teach me "the secrets of the ancients!" As I read the "effect" of trick after trick, I pictured in my mind what it would be like to be the audience as I performed these miracles. I couldn't believe I was going to be able to do these things!

However, reading the "method" of producing each "effect" produces a completely different experience. Every time I read the method, I was disappointed. I don't know quite what I was expecting, but I found most of the methods for how to do the tricks just weren't all that impressive.

I was riding a rollercoaster. I would read the "effect" of a new trick and be really excited about learning it, then I would read the "method" and be disappointed that it wasn't a real-life miracle. I would immediately discount the trick as something that wouldn't actually fool anyone.

So, I read, and I read, and I read some more. After a while, I finally made a list of a couple of card tricks with an impressive enough "effect" and "method" to try. I still wasn't convinced the tricks would fool anyone, but figured, "why not," and decided to try them out on my poker buddies.

At that Friday night's poker game, I decided to perform a trick called "The Betting Card Trick." It was designed to make it look to the audience like I had unknowingly failed. Then, at the very last second, I would turn the tables on everyone and successfully pull it off.

The reason it was called "The Betting Card Trick" was because it was designed and structured to make it look like I had failed so that everyone watching would be willing to bet me that I couldn't pull it off and be successful.

I performed the trick exactly as the instructions told me to. And when I came to the moment right before the end of the trick, I promised to reveal the right card and everyone at the table told me that I would fail. I said, "I'll bet you it will be the card," and my friends were diving for their wallets to make the bet.

When I revealed the correct card, there was a small roar from everyone at the table. To call it a thrill would be an understatement. At that moment, I knew that these "easy to do" card tricks were something special.

So, there I was, not long after that poker night, at the Abracadabra magic shop out by the Nashville International Airport. I was really interested in learning more card tricks, but was also fascinated by all the cool stuff that surrounded me.

I had no idea what any of this stuff did. I was truly a fish out of water. Fortunately for me, Garry Hayes, the gentleman who owned the shop, was very kind. After a few moments of me looking at all the stuff in the glass cases, Garry took charge and showed me several magic tricks that melted my brain.

Silk handkerchiefs magically changed color as he pushed them through his closed fist. Then, a few seconds later, those same hankies vanished into thin air, under test conditions.

Small red balls jumped from hand to hand. Then, somehow, those same red balls magically jumped into my hand!

I was seeing genuine miracles, up-close and personal, right in front of me. The crazy thing was that all this stuff was for sale. I could actually buy these miracles! And perform them!

As Garry hit me with magic trick after magic trick, I was having feelings of true astonishment. I remember wondering why I had never seen these things before. Here I was, sixteen years old, and I had never had a deeply impossible experience like the one I was having that day.

My next thought was, "I have to share this with other people. I have to do this so other people can have this same incredible experience that I'm having. I have to share this experience of the impossible with everyone I meet!"

I had stumbled onto my second defining moment.

CHAPTER FOUR

OVER THE NEXT six years, I had two passions: acting, and magic. Magic was really just a hobby for me. I put a huge amount of time into it, but it remained a hobby, none-theless. Acting was a whole different beast.

I had fallen in love with the stage and I was 100 percent focused on becoming a professional actor. I knew that was a million-to-one shot. I knew most actors were starving artists who spend a lot more time serving food and slinging drinks than acting, but I just knew, deep down, that I was different.

I enrolled in the invitation-only class "Performers" in my senior year of high school. That year was full of many more successful roles in school plays. I got major roles in every-thing that I went out for. I had found the thing that I was really, really good at.

And I continued to perform magic. My parents tapped into my new passion for magic when they asked me to perform a show for my sister's sixth birthday party. I performed magic at my church youth group. Basically, I would do magic for anyone who would watch.

What eluded me, however, was the practice of sleight-of-hand. I really didn't even know what sleight-of-hand was. I had always heard that the hand was faster than the eye. And since I wasn't naturally a very fast person, I thought that sleight-of-hand wasn't something I would be able to learn.

I knew that sleight-of-hand was supposed to be very difficult. I also knew that magic was an art form full of secrets and I really didn't feel very worthy of those secrets. Besides, I didn't know who in the world that I would talk to about learning the secrets in the first place.

But as the prophets say, when the student is ready, the teacher will appear. And a teacher did appear for a moment.

One Wednesday night with my family at a church dinner, I took out a little magic trick and started to show my parents. After I finished, a man walked up and introduced himself, saying he was a magician and asking if I wanted to see a trick. Well, of course I wanted to see a trick!

The man showed me a fantastic trick! Then he invited me to get together sometime if I wanted to talk magic. I couldn't believe it. This man lived in my community and he knew magic! More importantly, we were going to get together, and hopefully, he would teach me a few of those elusive "secrets."

I only saw that man a handful of times. It was so odd because I had been going to this church for almost ten years at that point in my life and I had never met, nor ever even seen this man before. He seemed to materialize from thin air for an

Doing a bit of magic early in my career.

instant in my life before vanishing back to where he came from.

But the few times that I did see him, I would show him the latest magic trick I had been working on and he would help me with it and then teach me something else to start practicing. The magic community is special like that. It is a very friendly group of men and women who understand that the best way to learn the art and craft is through personal instruction.

He and I never attacked the practice of sleight-of-hand together, but he did teach me several professional level tricks that I use to this day. I believe his role in my life was to open my eyes to learning a higher level of magic, and to open my mind to the possibility that I could in fact learn this elusive art form.

Unlike some of my favorite magic tricks, my Tourette's Syndrome hadn't vanished. By that point in my life, however, I had learned how to live with it. And that is to say that I had learned how to accept it.

Sometimes people wonder how I live with the tics and twitches they see me endure from time to time. I guess it's hard for them to imagine what it must be like to live in a body that sometimes appears to be completely out of control.

I don't know any other reality. The tics, twitches, and vocalizations are part of my life. As I explained, sometimes they wax and sometimes they wane. I may go for a time when the tics are very light and unnoticeable. Other times, the tics can be heavy and distracting to others. It's just part of my life.

It may be difficult to believe, but sometimes I might have a series of tics and twitches that I just don't even notice. Did they happen? Of course. Did I realize that I was having them? Not really.

One of the things that doctors tell children and teenagers with Tourette's Syndrome is that the majority of young people will grow out of the tics. For the most part, as they grow into adulthood, the twitches and vocalizations will fade away.

That news gives a lot of families and people who deal with the syndrome a lot of hope. "Just hold out long enough and, sooner or later, the hell that you are going through will subside." And as I grew older, the tics did in fact, start to fade.

When I was in college at Middle Tennessee State University, about an hour from home, I continued to seriously study acting while keeping magic as a hobby. A theatre major, I took every class I possibly could that would help me get more and more time onstage.

I went out for plays at my college as well as at community theatres in towns nearby. I wanted to work with as many people and play as many roles as possible. I was absolutely on fire when I was on stage. It didn't matter to me if I was playing a serious dramatic role or if I was getting laughs in a comedy. As long as I was on a stage somewhere, life was good.

The time I spent with the man from my church in high school must have fanned the flame that was smoldering inside of me for magic as well, because I began to become a frequent visitor to Abracadabra to pick up new tricks and see more magic.

I even decided to start visiting the Nashville Magic Club, which was a club of amateur, hobbyist, and professional magicians that met once a month in Nashville.

Attending those Nashville Magic Club meetings helped me get to know other local magicians. I met many knowledgeable magicians who were very giving with their time, knowledge, and a kind word.

One day, I was attending a party of some of my friends from church and I was asked to perform a couple of tricks. Well, like almost every budding magician, I had several tricks on me, and I was more than happy to comply.

So, I took out my deck of cards and proceeded to perform several tricks. I had several cards selected and located the cards by sense of touch. I found the four aces in the deck after it had been shuffled. It was pretty impressive stuff.

After I finished performing, one of the men from my church came up to me and told me that I had done a good job. He then said, "Yeah, you were using one of those shaved decks, weren't you? I used to have one of those, too."

My blood ran cold. He knew exactly how I had performed the supposed "miracles." I didn't know what to say, so I told him that he was right. I had, in fact, been using a special "magic" deck of cards.

The "shaved" deck of cards is a wonderful magic trick that is well within anyone's reach. With a little bit of practice and some basic card handling skills, you too could have performed the exact same miracles that I did.

Basically, the "shaved deck" is a special deck of cards that gives the performer the ability to simulate sleight-of-hand skills that would typically take years to master.

I was using the shaved deck because I couldn't perform sleight-of-hand. I thought it was too tough for me. I turned to special decks of cards that would do all the hard work, so I wouldn't have to.

What this man from my church had just unknowingly done was to call me out. He had ruined the pleasure I felt when I shared the feeling of deep amazement that magic creates.

He had taken away the joy of being able to execute a perfectly performed illusion. And while I didn't let anyone see my disappointment, I couldn't stop thinking about what had happened.

That was it. The gauntlet had been thrown down. I was never going to let a situation like that happen again. It was time to learn sleight-of-hand.

CHAPTER FIVE

THE NEXT WEEKEND I was back at Abracadabra, still doubting that I could learn sleight-of-hand, but not wanting to be called out again by someone who had dabbled in magic.

The glass cases full of interesting gadgets and gizmos still fascinated me, but my experience several days before caused those items to lose some of their luster. I found myself standing in front of several shelves full of books and videocassettes. I had never heard of any of these book authors. In fact, I really couldn't tell what half of the books were about since they were still in their plastic wrap.

As I perused the books that I could actually flip through, one of the other customers picked up a book titled <u>CardShark</u>. Garry, the shop's owner, called to him across the counter, "That's a really good book, there. It's tough, but really good."

As I read the back of one of the videotapes, I noticed the price. For about the same price of a good magic trick from the glass case I could buy a videocassette, or a book, that would teach me multiple tricks. Hmmm…

I was especially interested in a series of video tapes named "Easy to Master Money Miracles." I really liked the sound of "Easy to Master." That sounded like it was right up my alley. I had also seen a few of the guys around the magic shop do coin tricks and I was very impressed by them.

The description on the back of the box sold me on how easy it was to learn these "Money Miracles." Besides, I was going to learn eleven tricks from this tape, instead of only learning one from the glass case! I purchased it. Now it was time to get down to business.

If I thought that reading the "Effect" in a magic book and picturing what it would be like to experience the trick was thrilling, I had no words for how incredible it was to watch the world-class magician Michael Ammar perform these "Miracles" on this videotape.

The best part was that, after he performed money miracle after money miracle, he taught me how to do them! And Mr. Ammar was an excellent teacher.

These tricks really weren't that hard to do. They were certainly a little tougher than the card tricks from the <u>Scarne on Cards</u> book, but with a few minutes of dedicated practice I could do the tricks well enough to get me hooked on perfecting each of them.

Of course, the test of every great magic trick is whether it will fool your family. If Mom and Dad proclaimed, "How did you do that?" then I had a winner. Fortunately, the tricks on "Easy to Master Money Miracles" were all winners.

It didn't take long before I had purchased all three of the Money Miracle videotapes. And as I learned the different coin and money tricks in the series, I started to realize that learning sleight-of-hand wasn't as difficult as I had initially thought.

Now I trusted magic-teacher Michael Ammar. I trusted that, if he said it was "Easy to Master," then it was.

On my next trip to Abracadabra, I searched for what else was "Easy to Master." When I arrived back at the shelves full of books and videotapes, I saw that there was, in fact, another whole series of instructional tapes from Mr. Ammar titled, "Easy to Master Card Miracles."

I already knew how much I loved a good card trick. I also knew that if Michael Ammar said it was "Easy to Master," I believed him.

I returned home with my new instructional videocassette, and anxiously popped it into the VCR. A familiar feeling started to wash over me as I watched Michael's performance of the first couple of card tricks. I was revisiting "The Hook," which is that feeling of amazement responsible for getting so many young people interested in magic.

I got "hooked" when I walked into a magic shop for the first time, and now I was getting "hooked" even further as I watched these "Card Miracles." As Mr. Ammar finished his first couple of tricks on the videotape, I was all-in. I couldn't wait to learn these incredible card miracles.

Fortunately, the required sleight-of-hand expertise was well within my reach. After practicing the first two tricks on the videotape for several hours, I was ready to show them off to my family. And again, they amazed my Mom, Dad, brother, and sister.

My family really enjoyed the magic that I shared with them and they were always very supportive. In fact, one of my favorite memories of being a young magician occurred one evening when my brother Brian had several friends at my house for a sleepover and he asked me to come entertain his friends with "a few things."

There is no better feeling in the world than perfectly executing a well-designed magic trick. That night I performed several great card tricks from the videotape for my brother's friends to great reactions. The coup de grace, however, occurred when I performed my favorite trick, "Red Hot Mama."

I had saved it for last because I knew it was the best trick I knew. "Red Hot Mama" was also one of the very first tricks I had learned from the latest tape. It was a perfectly designed trick that had multiple layers of magic that climaxed in a moment of complete shock and deep amazement. And I performed it perfectly for my brother's friend Charlie.

When Charlie turned over the card that I had placed in his hand a moment before, he jumped up from the table, threw the card down, and started to scream as he ran out of my parent's house and down the driveway!

I didn't know what to do! I was as shocked by Charlie's reaction as he was by "Red Hot Mama." Had I done something I shouldn't have? No one had ever reacted so strongly to one of my tricks. But when Charlie came walking back down the driveway still freaked out and talking about the trick, my brother and all his friends couldn't stop laughing and talking about it too.

I was on cloud nine! Charlie's reaction and my brother's other friends' reactions gave me one of the highest highs I had ever experienced. Now "The Hook" was deeply set.

I visited Abracadabra many weekends looking for the latest, greatest tricks I could learn and share with my friends and family. Every time I went in there, I saw the book that shop owner Garry had said was so good, the one titled "CardShark."

The idea of being a CardShark really appealed to me. So, one day I picked the book up and started to thumb through it. What you must understand is that reading a book on sleight-of-hand is akin to reading Braille while standing on your head, underwater. Or, at the very least, it feels like you are reading a different language.

Most books on sleight-of-hand are written like technical manuals. They outline very specific instructions on how to hold the playing cards, finger placement for different techniques, and the proper choreography of movements and gestures to successfully create the illusion you are aiming at.

As I tried to decipher all the instructions and pictures I was looking at, I started to think that maybe this wasn't the book for me. This appeared to be the "sleight-of-hand" that I knew was so difficult. This was the stuff that I had known for years that I wouldn't be able to do. But I kept looking through the book. I just couldn't put it down.

I finally found myself reading the description of a trick titled "Against All Odds." The "Effect" was really appealing to me, so I read on. In the "method" section, the author, Darwin Ortiz, mentioned that this was probably the easiest trick in the book and that anyone should be able to do it.

Easy? Well, I knew that, if it was "easy," then I could, at least, learn that one. And maybe I might find something else in there that I could learn. So I bought the book.

I quickly found out that Garry was right about the book being "tough." It was tough, really tough. There were sleight-of-hand techniques in this book that I would never be able to do.

Here I put on a performance for a church audience.

But there were several tricks that were intermediate level that I could, in fact, learn. So I set myself to learning them.

"CardShark" turned out to be one of the best purchases I could have made. Because different tricks in the book used different sleight-of-hand techniques, I was constantly challenged. The tricks in the book were, quite literally, world-class. And because I was motivated to learn the different tricks I found myself learning lots of new sleight-of-hand techniques.

I continued my study of sleight-of-hand as I finished up my course of study in theatre upon graduating from Middle Tennessee State University. Now I had to figure out what I was going to do next.

I originally planned to move to Los Angeles or New York City after I graduated to pursue an acting career. Now I wasn't so sure that was the right thing to do. So, I stayed put in middle Tennessee while I tried to figure out the next career move.

Over the next year, I had several jobs. I left a job that I had enjoyed during my college years with a family entertainment center and worked as a loan processor/administrative assistant for a mortgage company. And as nice as the people were, that just wasn't my thing. I also took a sales job with a cellular phone company.

My Tourette's still waxed and waned from time to time, but my twenties mostly brought the peace and stillness from the tics that the doctors had promised when I was a child.

I continued to dabble in theatre and participate in small shows in the community. The one thing that really stayed constant for me, though, was the art of magic. One day I was sitting on my bed, reading Magic Magazine, and I turned the page to see a half-page ad seeking technical assistants and onstage helpers/performers for a major illusion show in Tunica, Mississippi.

I had been to Tunica. It was only about four hours away from my house. In fact, I had seen this show! Brett Daniels' show "Magique" was at one of the nicest casino resorts in Tunica, The GoldStrike. And it was a great show! I had seen several grand-illusion shows in the last few years and "Magique" was one of my favorites! I immediately put together my theatre resume and sent it to the show's production manager.

Several days went by before my phone rang. When I answered, I was speaking to a man named Peter Bryant who was Magique's production manager. Peter told me he had received my resume and wanted to meet me. He asked me several questions about my experience, told me a little bit about what they were looking for, and then invited me to Tunica to see the show and meet Brett Daniels.

I was excited! I had a really good shot at working for Brett Daniels in his big-time illusion show in a casino resort. Whoa!

Brett Daniels was one of my heroes. While not a major celebrity in the general public's eye, Brett was absolutely a superstar in the world of magic and illusion. Just a few years before, when I had been in college, I had been introduced to

Brett by the annual television special "The World's Greatest Magic."

"The World's Greatest Magic" was a network television show that was on every year from 1994 to 1998 during the Thanksgiving holiday. And Brett was, by far, my favorite performer on that show. Brett had that indefinable quality that so few entertainers have. He had "it." On "The World's Greatest Magic," he had a charisma and magnetism that you just couldn't turn away from. I couldn't tell you how many times I watched that show just to watch his segments.

My friend Jeff and I travelled down to Tunica on a Tuesday afternoon. We checked in at The GoldStrike and got a bite to eat as we waited for that evening's show. That night we excitedly made our way into the Millennium Theatre.

The Millennium Theatre at The GoldStrike Casino was a beautiful, large theatre, rivaling any of the performing arts centers I had been in to see other shows. When I walked into it, I felt like I was walking into a vast, giant, cold chasm. It was very, very large, but had the feel of being in a cave.

Brett's show was fantastic! I knew it was going to be, and Brett didn't disappoint. After the show I met Peter and he asked me to stick around for a few minutes to talk to Brett. I was in awe. This was the guy who had been on "The World's Greatest Magic." This was the guy who was the star of the incredible illusion show that I had just seen.

When I met Brett, I told him how much I enjoyed the show and he asked me if I wanted to play a part in it. I said that I did. He and Peter explained that my job would be to work on the backstage team with many of the illusions and, from time to time, be onstage helping out. I told them that I could do it. They offered me the job.

As I walked out of the theatre with Peter, he asked me if I could start that Sunday. Wow, that was in five days! That was fast! I told him that I could. I was so excited I probably would have agreed to almost anything.

That week was a whirlwind of activity. The first thing I had to do was to go tell my manager at the cell phone store that I was quitting in three days. I really didn't like not giving them a two-week notice, but I also knew that I wasn't going to jeopardize an opportunity like the one I was getting with Brett over a formality like a two-week notice.

Next, I had to get a reliable car. So, I bought my friend's car that he had just decided to sell. Finally, I had to say "See ya later!" to my friends and family.

My decision shocked my family a little, for making a major life-decision like the one I had just made wasn't usually done so fast. But then again, getting the opportunity to work for a big-time illusionist wasn't very usual either. They trusted my judgment and knew I would be okay.

Now all I had to do was see as many of my friends as possible before I left.

I met my buddy, Aarron, as a college freshman. We both went out for roles in the children's play my college staged and we both got a part. He and I had been friends ever since. I called Aarron, and several other friends, and told them that we had to get together for a big night out before I left town a few days later.

That Friday night, we all headed to Second Avenue in downtown Nashville, where the nightlife all went down. There were eight to ten of us and we visited all the hot spots.

At one point in the evening, we were sitting at the Havana Lounge having a few laughs when Aarron turned to me and told me that I had to go up and do magic for a large table of ladies in a bachelorette party. In addition to being a good friend, challenging me to do magic is what Aarron was really good at.

As hard as this may be to understand, I am a naturally shy person. Yes, I could get up in front of a crowd and perform in a show. And yes, I could do magic tricks for friends and family. But just walking up to a group of strangers, introducing myself, and launching into a bunch of magic tricks… yeah, that wasn't going to happen.

But Aarron had been up to something over the last year. Every time he and I went out for a night on the town, he would always make sure that I had a deck of cards in my pocket. Then he would turn to a person sitting at the bar next to us, or at an adjacent table, and tell them that I was a great close-up magician. Then he basically told them that I was going to do some magic for them.

I constantly found myself in situations where I was performing card tricks and sleight-of-hand magic for complete strangers. At first, it was a terrifying experience. But as we went out more and more often, I started to hope that he would "pimp me out." I didn't want to be the one asking if I could do magic tricks for complete strangers, but I got a huge thrill and a major boost in confidence each time it happened.

So now Aarron had thrown down the gauntlet in front of all my other buddies, "Go do some magic for that table full of hot chicks!" Two emotions sprung up inside me: excitement to do magic for a bunch of beautiful women who I wanted to impress, and terror over the idea that I had to walk up to a table full of beautiful women and try to do magic for them!

The way I saw it was that I had nothing to lose. I was leaving to move to Tunica in two days, so who really cared if I crashed and burned?

I made my way over to the table of women and introduced myself. When I explained that I was a magician, one of the young ladies really perked up, so I focused on her. I performed my first trick, Red Hot Mama, and got a huge reaction. It wasn't as big as the time I performed it for Charlie at my parent's house, but the women were now definitely interested in what I was doing.

My friends made their way over to the table as I transitioned into my next trick. I turned to the bride to be and asked her if she would like to participate. She said she would. For the next few minutes I involved many of the ladies in the bachelorette party in my sleight-of-hand as my friends made friends with the rest of the ladies.

After I finished performing, the women invited all of us to follow them down the street to another bar where they were headed. I had done it! I had successfully approached a table full of strangers, beautiful women strangers, that is, and won them over with magic. And then they invited us all to hang out with them. This had been an amazing week, full of milestones!

Two days later it was Sunday. I had told my friends to come and visit and see the show in Tunica. I had told my family that I would keep them updated on all the latest news and that I would call as soon as I got there. And I had packed my new Mustang full of clothing and personal stuff and was heading to Tunica to join the cast and crew of Brett Daniel's show "Magique" that evening.

As I drove west towards Tunica, I had nowhere to stay the night, very little money, and no clue of what adventures this new job might open up for me. What I did know, however, was that I was going to learn how to do "the impossible!"

CHAPTER SIX

ILLUSIONISTS ARE THE performers in the magic fraternity who get credit for doing the impossible. Think about it. They make people appear and disappear. They cut beautiful women in half and put them back together. They do some pretty amazing illusions. And I was going to work for one of the best.

I arrived at The Gold Strike Casino right on time. I was assigned to shadow and learn everything that Joe taught me. Joe was the guy whose place I was taking.

When I met Joe that day, he told me to pay very close attention to everything he said because he was going to be leaving the show and heading north as soon as I was up to speed. To say that I paid close attention would be an understatement. I was locked in. Whatever Joe said, I was totally focused on and taking notes. He went into a lot of detail for my first day on the job.

The first hour was spent on taking care of "pre-sets" — the setting up of each illusion so that it was prepared to be executed during the show. And there was a whole team of guys doing "pre-sets." That's how large and impressive Brett Daniels' grand illusion show was.

When it was time for the show, I followed Joe around and did my best to take everything in. To say that it was "unbelievable" backstage might be putting it lightly. I wish everyone could experience what it is like to watch a large illusion show from the backstage area. Dancers run on and off stage, guys move large equipment into and out of position onstage, and general mayhem reigns, in addition to the actual show that is occurring out in front of the audience. Let's just say that it was eye-opening.

I did my best to learn as much as possible while shadowing Joe during the show. There was a ton to learn. I quickly figured out that Joe had a lot of very important cues to take care of both on and off the stage. He was one of the unseen, incredibly important guys who helped create the illusions that were taking place for the audience.

After the show was over, I sat in the post-show meeting and tried to take everything in. I figured it would take me at least a week to get up to speed and I hoped to be completely integrated into the show by the end of the two weeks before Joe was scheduled to head out.

After the meeting, one of the guys from the crew named Mike came up to me and asked where I was staying. I told him I had no clue. In my excitement, I hadn't really thought about it. He told me that I could stay at his house for a while until I figured something out. So I followed Mike home.

The next day, Monday, was the show's day off. Mostly, I sat around and asked Mike questions about what I would need to know to get up to speed. While we were chatting, Mike got a call from Peter. As I listened to Mike talk to Peter the conversation started to take a serious tone. When Mike hung up, he turned to me and said that Peter was coming over.

When Peter arrived, I learned that Joe had vanished in the night. Apparently, when Joe told me to pay close attention, he actually was saying I needed to learn his job in a day. Joe had gotten fed up with the show and he headed home as soon as he had a suitable replacement.

Let's just say that Peter was a bit nervous. As production manager, his job was to make sure that the show went off without a hitch night after night. Now he had lost a very valuable member of his team. He had a replacement right here in front of him, but Peter knew I hadn't learned all that I needed to know to do Joe's job. Or so he thought.

As I listened to Peter tell me that we had to figure out a way to do Tuesday night's show, I was strangely calm. The way I figured it, I had plenty of training. I had performed in and participated in shows constantly for the last nine years. I wasn't being asked to do anything that I couldn't do. In fact, I took the job precisely so that I could learn all of this stuff. I was just being asked to learn it in an accelerated timeframe.

Peter looked at me like I was a little bit crazy when I told him that we would be fine. I told him that I just needed to get to the theatre early Tuesday morning to take a crash course from the other guys on everything that I absolutely had to do that night.

At 10 a.m. Tuesday morning, I was standing onstage of the GoldStrike Resort with all the other guys on the crew and several of the dancers. I had to learn how to properly execute seven different illusions. And these weren't small things to learn. These were big things. In these seven illusions, I was personally responsible for the illusion's success or failure. I was the guy onstage that everyone was looking directly at, but no one saw.

In addition to learning how to operate these illusions under fire, I also had to learn how to drive a large, very heavy motorcycle, with only a few hours to learn. After all, the motorcycle illusion was one of the most important illusions in the show.

I'd never driven a motorcycle and had no idea how one worked. So the guys started at the beginning. I learned about the clutch, shifting gears, and how to ride. By mid-afternoon, I could drive the motorcycle well enough so that I wouldn't lay it down on the stage or drive it into the audience.

As the day passed and I reviewed everything I needed to know, the guys on the stage crew (Mike, Tim, Donovan, Chris, and Dan) made it very clear that they would take up my slack. They just wanted me to focus on making sure that I could pull off the illusions.

It's all or nothing with a magic or an illusion show. There is no in-between. The audience comes to see magic and illusions that appear to be completely impossible. If the magician doesn't successfully pull off the tricks, the show fails and the audience leaves disappointed.

Well, I wasn't about to fail Brett, my new team, or the audience. I was totally fired up that night at show time, the adrenaline running high and my senses in overdrive.

And then the music started, the lights dimmed, and the show began, with everything a bit of a blur. Dancers came onstage, large props moved around me, and the guys bounced all over the place doing their jobs.

As I stood on the side of the stage gathering my bearings, I had several trump cards to play. My very detailed notes told me where to go and what to do backstage; I had rehearsed earlier in the day with the cast and crew, and a great team of guys around me pointed me in the right direction at the right times.

Suddenly, I was onstage doing my job. As the show progressed, I either wore a costume and participated in the illusion sequence, or I was hidden away, unseen by the audience, assisting in the execution of the illusion.

And then it was time for the big moment — time to drive the motorcycle to its spot onstage so that it could vanish in a flash of fire and smoke. This illusion sequence was timed to the music and the cycle would vanish at a very specific second, then reappear several seconds later in a moment of eye-popping amazement!

I mounted the cycle totally focused on driving it to its exact spot onstage without crashing. And then one of the show's dancers, Jamie, got on the back of the cycle to ride with me. Whoa! No pressure!

I got the motorcycle into its position, did all the necessary things that had to be done in order to make the cycle vanish successfully, then all I had to do was wait — for the cycle to be raised into the air about thirty feet. That's right; the motorcycle would vanish while suspended in mid-air!

Once the cycle got to the correct height, I listened carefully to the music. At the proper second, I pulled the trigger and there was a loud boom. As the pyrotechnics exploded in a flash of fire, the motorcycle melted into thin air. It was beautiful!

Now all I had to do was get down from my perch about thirty feet above the stage. To do that, I had to drop a rope from my hidden position with the motorcycle thirty feet above the stage and free rappel to the stage floor. Yeah, that's right... free rappelling was another new skill I had to learn that day.

So, dangling in the air with nothing to hold on to but a rope thirty feet above the stage, I had to slide down without falling and breaking my neck. I safely slid down and met Donovan, one of the crew guys, standing at the bottom of the rope. He told me the motorcycle illusion had gone perfectly.

I had already been above the stage. Now it was time to finish off the show by participating in an incredible multi-illusion sequence that had me underneath the stage, running down dark corridors, up ladders, and on both sides of the stage, as well as being on the stage.

Everything went off without a hitch. A few moments later, as Brett and the dancers were taking their bows, I was catching my breath as the crew guys gave me pats on the back for a job well done.

I had done it, and I had done it in a day. With one day of training, I had learned how to perform and execute all of the major illusion sequences in the show. I had learned how to drive and vanish a huge motorcycle, and I did it in that night's show. I had learned how to rappel as I hung freely thirty feet above the stage. I had been tested under fire, and I had learned that I could, in fact, do the impossible.

CHAPTER SEVEN

WORKING FOR BRETT Daniels was one of the great experiences of my life. It came at the perfect moment in time and I was surrounded by talented, hardworking people who became close friends.

I worked in Brett's show until the contract ended at the end of 2000. I stuck around Tunica for another year bartending at the Grand Casino & Resort trying to figure out what to do next.

What I did next was to write my own show. Every night I bartended at the Grand and every day I spent time writing a show script. And while my show script wasn't particularly sophisticated, it proved to be an excellent exercise in creating a show starting at the most basic, conceptual level.

As much as I enjoyed bartending and being around all my friends in Tunica and Southaven, Mississippi, I knew I needed to return to Nashville to turn my script into a fully produced show.

I returned to my home of Nashville in 2002 and took a job at a local restaurant bartending. I really enjoyed bartending, but

I knew that I didn't want to make it my career. At the time, it provided the perfect job while I transitioned into the next part of my life. It allowed me to make some quick money while I figured out how to take all of the training I had in the magic and theatre worlds and turn those skills into a full-time job as a magician.

After all, I had big goals. I had a degree in theatre. I had also worked for Brett Daniels, one of the top illusionists in the world. I had even written my own show. I had more training than just about every other magician I had ever heard of. The way I saw it: if anyone was ever qualified to be a magician, I definitely topped the list.

While I worked at the restaurant, I continued to practice sleight-of-hand. I had again cracked open the book "Card-Shark" and was working hard learning new interactive, close-up mysteries. Very soon, I started to incorporate card tricks and other magic at the bar in between mixing drinks.

I loved performing magic behind the bar. And while I didn't have a show behind the bar, I did have some fantastic close-up magic that never failed to 'wow' everyone watching. Besides, working for real people in an intimate, interactive setting provided an education in itself.

It quickly became evident to me that, if I wanted my career as a big-time stage magician to take off, I would have to be the one driving it forward. So I did what I knew best. I returned to the theatre.

As I continued bartending, I also began to create, purchase, and practice all the magic that would be in my show. I then began contacting local theatres in the middle Tennessee area. Through creativity and sheer force of will, I worked out deals with small colleges, community theatres, and arts centers to use their stages.

My first official show on the calendar came at the Lakewood Community Theatre in Lakewood, TN. I had seen numerous shows at the Lakewood Theatre, a small venue that sat about 80 people comfortably, and I was familiar with the space.

Now all I had to do was hire an assistant, find a crew, rehearse the entire team, get an opening act, advertise the show, sell tickets, and perform it. It sounded like a normal day at the theatre to me. Little did I realize at the time, but I was earning my stripes as a producer, too.

Creating and staging a show requires a ton of hard work. In fact, just about every show I have ever been a part of reaches a point when everyone looks at each other and wonders aloud why we put ourselves through the craziness.

The hours are long, most of the tasks far from glamorous, the pay isn't usually very good, and the long breaks in between work can be deeply depressing. Then the show elements start coming together, all the strangers become a little family, and you start seeing your efforts start to take shape.

The act of creating a show is deeply rewarding and is forged through the pressure of deadlines, the unforgiving spotlight, and the hope of a grateful, applauding audience. It is a drug like no other.

It had been several years since the tics of my Tourette's Syndrome had really been very strong. Sure, they had waxed and waned, but they had been very mild most of the time. But with high-pressure situations like producing your own magic show come a great deal of stress. And with a great deal of stress come tics and twitches.

I never know quite how the tics will manifest themselves. I've had vocal tics that sounded like I was constantly clearing my throat. And I've made odd noises that sounded like a clicking noise that I made with my mouth and tongue. I've even had tics that had obsessive-compulsive qualities that force me to read the same sentence over and over and over again in a book. Perhaps the most constant tic for me, though, has been the one that popped back up during the preparation for the Lakewood show.

This tic would affect my head and, sometimes, my left arm and shoulder. I would rapidly twitch my head to the left over and over again while my left shoulder and arm raised up in the air several inches. The tic would happen most frequently when I wore a shirt with a collar, or a shirt tight around my neck. There's something about having any sort of fabric against my neck that fires off this tic. In other words, you can forget about me ever wearing a tie.

Additionally, it's a pretty violent and distracting tic. I can be busy doing something and this tic can completely shut down everything else that my body is doing while it forces its way out of my body. I'm sure it's quite a sight to the people around me.

As opening night for my show at Lakewood grew closer, a typical day might look like this: practice and rehearse during the day, bartend at the restaurant in the evenings, and try not to be noticed as I twitched and ticked in my down time.

Fortunately, as always, when it was time to take the stage in front of a living and breathing audience, the tics vanished like a magic trick. All my shows at Lakewood Theatre drew great audiences and I got that shot in the arm needed to keep my energy level high and push the show forward.

Over the next several months, I staged several shows in and around Nashville. I had become quite the show producer. Between the media appearances, the press releases, and the constant hustle, I sold quite a few tickets and managed to make some money.

I was on a roll. The show was starting to get some traction and building a buzz. When I wasn't performing a public show on the weekend I still tended bar at the restaurant. And then it happened...I got the phone call from Brett to go to China.

CHAPTER EIGHT

Brett had just signed the contract on a multi-city tour that started with six weeks in Shanghai, China. I had never been out of the country. Now I was going halfway around the world to perform Brett's illusion show for a country that proved to be hungry for a spectacular magic show.

Brett built his team from dancers and members of his crew in Tunica. We also had several new dancers joining our show family. So everyone made their way to Brett's home in Memphis, TN. Every day we drove from Brett's house about an hour into Mississippi and rehearsed inside a swelteringly hot warehouse where all the props and equipment were stored in the late months of summer.

Several weeks later, we boarded a jumbo jet and flew eighteen hours west to Shanghai. We arrived five or six days early to get the show from the shipyard, move it into the arena, build it, go through technical rehearsals, and get fully up to speed.

My first impression of China was quite a bit different than I expected. As we drove through the city from the airport, I was shocked to find Shanghai to be a concrete jungle, a huge, cosmopolitan city full of western restaurants, coffee houses, and English speaking nationals everywhere!

After a fitful night's sleep at our hotel, the next day we went to the arena where Brett's show would play and got right to work. For several days, Brett, the crew, and the dancers went about our business efficiently and effectively. We built props and prepared show equipment. Costumes got unpacked and steamed. We started technical rehearsals.

Getting used to the time difference poses one of the big challenges of staging a show halfway across the world, because daytime in China is nighttime in the United States. When we finished each day of work, we struggled to sleep as our bodies tried to adapt to this new time zone. We weren't getting a lot of rest, but everything was going to plan. And then it happened, the day before opening night — we hit an unforeseen brick wall.

We had spent the last two days getting somewhere between three and four hours of fitful sleep each night while we got all the lights focused in their correct spots and programmed into the computerized lighting board.

Basically, in order to light a large illusion show, you have to go from cue to cue with the light board operator and program in which lights are on and which lights are off for every single cue. As you go through this crazy long process, you also ensure that the lights are focused properly and aren't giving away any of the secrets. This also means that all of the performers must be onstage during the entire process to make sure the lights illuminate everyone correctly.

Having finished lighting the show late the night before, we returned to the arena to get ready to go through our first rehearsal. As we started the rehearsal, we quickly noticed that none of the lighting cues were being hit. All the performers and technicians were in the right spots in the right moments, but the lights didn't look anything like they were supposed to look.

I first thought we would have to put a translator at the light board to help the operator know when each cue was supposed to happen. But things started to get weird when Brett asked the guy to show us the first light cue. When he pulled up the first cue, it didn't look anything like it looked when we initially programmed it a few days before. The same was true with the second and third light cues. This didn't make any sense.

We finally figured out that the light board operator had been making manual notes of which lights were supposed to be on at which times and he expected to turn on each light manually at the proper moment. In other words, he hadn't programmed the light board at all! And this was for a grand illusion show that had more than a hundred light cues with dozens of lights on and others off during each cue!

Keep in mind that we had spent days programming the light board with the correct cues and the show was scheduled to open, basically, the next day! I thought I was going to lose my mind because I knew what this meant...

You see, when you are in an arena in China and a lot of people (including the government) have spent a lot of money, you are going to open the show on the date that you have set. There isn't any room for negotiation.

In any normal world, we would have postponed our start date and spent the next several days re-programming the light board. In the crazy world of China, we had a day to get the show launched successfully. So what did that look like, you ask?

I'll tell you what it looked like. It looked like we got zero sleep that night after we were already suffering from sleep deprivation. We also got no time to rehearse the show. We spent that full day and night re-lighting the show with the light board operator, and he actually programmed the board this time!

The day we opened the show passed in something of a blur. Delirious from getting no sleep, everyone had tons of little details still to take care of. We got a cue-to-cue rehearsal in with the lighting guy so that he would have us, more or less, in the right lighting cues in the right moments.

That afternoon, several hours before the show, we were all looking at each other, seeing a roomful of zombies, and it seemed we had zero chance of having a successful show. It just seemed impossible.

We hadn't slept more than ten hours in the last three days. With the lighting debacle, our team lost any chance to re-hearse. To be honest, I could barely think straight. Fortunately, Brett Daniels had assembled a team of talented, dedicated, determined artists and technicians determined to do everything in our power to succeed.

Here I am on tour standing in front of a China stadium.

That night, when the arena filled full of dignitaries, special guests, VIPs, and audience members, the adrenaline started to flow because we knew this was our moment of truth. We had flown halfway across the world and spent nearly a week preparing. If this show didn't go well, the whole tour was at stake.

Our rallying cry, and the thing that pushed us through our deliriousness, was something that I had said the day before we opened when we learned that the lighting had to be completely redone.

We were all standing around in a circle having a very frustrating conversation. Everyone basically agreed there was no way to succeed. Our morale sagged and the challenge of getting the show launched successfully looked impossible.

As we were discussing what our next steps should be, I felt like we were being tested. We had two months of shows in front of us if we could succeed in getting the show up and running. Though exhausted, the thought of giving up made me sick. Even though it seemed far, far away, I could see the finish line in sight.

I gathered everyone together and proclaimed, "Let's knock this b!tch out!" After all, I was excited to be experiencing China for the next two months. I was going to do everything in my power to make sure we had a tour!

And that's exactly what we did — we knocked that b!tch out! When the lights dimmed and the show music started, I knew if we could survive the next ninety minutes, we were in good shape for the next several months.

Was the show perfect that night? Probably not. But was it an outstanding show considering that it felt utterly impossible to do the day before? Absolutely!

Little did I know at the time, but this experience amounted to another defining moment for me. We all knew Brett was the boss. It was his show. The rest of us were on his team. We really didn't have a "crew chief." Everyone on the team did their part to make the show work. If someone was slacking off or unable to fulfill their job, the rest of us came together and made the show work.

However, I was the technician who had been around the longest. And while I didn't actively seek out any sort of special title or ask for a promotion, the other guys started to look at me as a leader.

My first trip to China with Brett lasted about two and a half months and I learned a great deal about myself. We spent the first six weeks in Shanghai then took the show to several other major cities in China that I had never heard of.

Being that far away from home provides an eye-opening experience. I learned how to be self-reliant very quickly, which is an excellent leadership quality. After all, when things on the tour didn't go well, our team didn't have the option of turning to someone else to take care of our problems.

We were there to do a show and that show had to happen at each venue on time, every time. It didn't matter if I'd had a bad day or if the odds appeared to be stacked against us.

A bit of sleight-of-hand on one of my tours in China.

I'm reminded of what it was like to finish our show in each city and immediately having to tear down all the props and pack them in their cases. We then had to load multiple trucks full of cases and equipment throughout what turned into very long nights.

It was normal for us to finish our show at 10 p.m. and be working until 6 a.m. the next morning as we got everything prepared to move to the next city.

During those long nights, I continually reminded myself at 3 or 4 in the morning that we could, in fact, get the job done. And every time we moved a big case of equipment out of the theatre and into the truck, I imagined what the theatre would look like in a few hours when the place was completely empty, just the way we found it.

I knew that, as long as we kept moving forward, loading heavy case after heavy case, we would get to that glorious picture in my mind, sitting in the bus, looking back at an empty theatre, as we drove away, having been triumphant in our show the night before.

As I think about that experience in China, I realize the importance of that tour in my development as a person and as a leader.

The biggest thing I learned, which helped me tremendously throughout the rest of my life, was that I could accomplish anything. I learned that, no matter how big the challenge at any point in time, I could attack it head-on and come out victorious. I learned that, when I am facing something that looks truly impossible to overcome, I should lower my shoulders, walk firmly into the fire, and "knock that b!tch out"!

CHAPTER NINE

WHEN I RETURNED home from my adventures in China, going back to work as a bartender at the restaurant didn't excite me anymore. I needed to figure out the next step in my career. Fortunately, Brett scheduled another tour of China several months later and I made my break with the restaurant.

The second tour of China passed much like the first. Our team overcame challenges, had lots of adventures, and put on a great show. Two months later, I returned home and realized I was now officially in business for myself.

I remember sitting at my computer a few days after I returned home, and thinking to myself, "Now you are officially a magician. You're on your own and you're open for business." My very next thought: "But nobody knows that. Hmmm… how do I get the word out and try to get some business?"

The immediate answer was to turn to my sleight-of-hand skills. I knew that I had a good show, but a show designed for theatre spaces, not private parties. My card tricks and other close-up magic, however, could work anywhere, at any function. So, I picked up the phone and started making some calls.

My first call went to the restaurant where I had bartended. After all, they knew exactly what it was like to have me performing magic for their guests. I scheduled a meeting with the manager and pitched myself as a strolling magician one or two days a week.

Apparently, my magic had been a hit, because the manager liked my idea and scheduled me to start coming in once a week to perform tableside as guests waited for their food to arrive. I was officially on my way with my first recurring gig and a little bit of money coming in every week. Now all I had to do was start booking some private parties and corporate functions.

Little by little, I started to build my business over the next six months. It was slow going. Oh, I knew all about the theatre world and how to stage a successful show, but I had zero knowledge of the business world and how to market and sell myself as a professional entertainer.

But what I lacked in knowledge I certainly made up for in persistence. I knew that one of the best ways to start getting additional business was to build my visibility in the greater middle Tennessee area. So, I purchased a book that taught me how to write a press release and I started targeting local newspapers and television stations.

One of the things the book taught me was that you needed a timely hook to get the media's attention. I knew that pitching myself as a local guy who became a professional magician might get some attention from the press because it was so unique. But I also knew that I had to keep hammering the media with different angles to continue getting news coverage.

In late September, I was trying to figure out how to get some Christmas and holiday party bookings when I realized that Halloween was only about six weeks away. I also knew that Halloween is a very timely hook for magicians, because Harry Houdini, the most famous magician and escape artist of all time, died on Halloween in 1926.

I thought that I could almost guarantee some great press coverage if I could orchestrate a stunt that focused on Houdini's life and death on Halloween. And that is when I had a crazy idea.

In 2003, Opry Mills Mall, Nashville's newest mall, had only been open a few years. So, I hit on the idea of staging "The Houdini Challenge" on October 31st. "The Houdini Challenge" would be a free show open to the public that would build a large crowd at the mall that evening.

I would perform only illusions and magic tricks at "The Houdini Challenge" that Harry Houdini had performed in his magic shows eighty years ago. As a huge fan of Houdini, I already had a small repertoire of tricks and illusions from my show that I knew would be a big hit. Now all I needed was something spectacular to make the event newsworthy.

I knew what I had to do. I had to go way out of my comfort zone and ask Brett if I could borrow one of the props from his show. Brett had one specific piece of equipment in his warehouse that I knew would virtually guarantee news coverage — Houdini's Water Torture Cell.

Harry Houdini invented the Water Torture Cell, and featured the act in his show for years. In the escape, Houdini's crew locked his ankles into stocks, and hoisted him into the air by the stocks until he hung upside down suspended by his ankles.

He would then be lowered into an upright cell filled with water that looked a great deal like a

Here I demonstrate the set-up for the Water Torture Cell, shown behind me.

phone booth. The stocks were locked to the top of the cell and onlookers watched Houdini try to free himself from the Water Cell through its glass walls.

A dangerous and extremely difficult escape, the Water Torture Cell was only marginally safe in a professionally trained escape artist's hands. So dammit, that's what I was going to do.

I had partnered with my friend John and he and I had already met with and sold "The Houdini Challenge" to the mall. Now I had to call Brett and see if I could borrow his Underwater Torture Cell.

Even though I had worked with Brett hand-in-hand for years and was happy to call him a friend, I still had some hero worship going on. This was the guy who had starred in all those television shows. He'd had his own show in a major casino. He'd toured all over the world. Why in the world would he let me borrow some of the equipment from his multi-million-dollar show?

The phone call to Brett turned out to be a lot easier than I had thought it would be. When I told him what I wanted to do, he was happy to let me use the Underwater Torture Cell. In fact, he spent quite a bit of time talking to me about the finer points of performing the escape. Brett shared tips and techniques with me about how to escape from it that only would be known by someone with a great deal of personal experience.

I knew I had built up trust and professional respect with him when he kindly let me borrow the equipment and took the time to educate me about it as well. It gave me another nice shot in the arm that I needed. If Brett trusted me to do it, I knew that I could.

So, I rented a U-Haul truck and made my way from Nashville to Mississippi where Brett stored all of his show equipment. After an afternoon of moving large road cases and heavy equipment, I got the Water Torture Cell loaded into the U-Haul and on its way back to middle Tennessee.

As I unloaded the water torture cell into my parent's garage late that night, it quickly became clear to me that I would be dealing with a lot more logistical issues than I first envisioned.

The Water Torture Cell is designed in a way to create an impressive image in the audiences mind. Because it is built like a phone booth, it is tall and slender with the opening at the top of the prop. That means the performer must enter the cell from above. And since Houdini designed the cell for maximum shock, the escape artist hangs upside down by his or her ankles and is lowered head-first into the cell. That means that, in order to practice and perform it, a hoist has to be positioned at the top of a super high ceiling.

Well, my parent's garage did not have a high ceiling and my bank account didn't have enough money in it for me to rent a rehearsal space. So that meant that I would rehearse escaping from the cell in a very creative manner.

Over the next several weeks, my friends Aarron and Fred spent the evenings with me in my parent's garage as I practiced and learned the finer points of Houdini's Water Torture Cell.

Here are a few things I learned. When you fill a large tank with water from the garden hose in the middle of October in middle Tennessee, that water is going to be cold! It may not feel that cold to the touch, but it's going to freeze your buns off when you have to fully immerse yourself upside down in it. And ridiculously cold water takes your breath away and makes it very hard to hold your breath for any serious length of time.

I had been working on holding my breath from the day I called Brett and asked to borrow the cell. Here is how gung-ho (and slightly crazy) I was. I knew that I had to be able to hold my breath for at least a minute and a half in order to give myself enough time to escape without putting my life in danger or having to destroy the torture cell by breaking the front glass wall and letting the water rush out. And, to be honest, a minute and a half was the bare minimum. Realistically, I needed to be able to hold my breath for more like two-and-a-half minutes.

So, every morning I made my way down to the local YMCA with my swimsuit in my bag and I swam. I swam laps while holding my breath for as long as possible, and then, at the end of my workout, I would rest my legs on the side of the pool as I took huge breaths of air until I leaned back into the pool so that I would be head first, upside-down, trying to simulate the water torture cell.

Little by little, I made progress. When I started, I couldn't hold my breath very long at all, maybe 30 seconds. But as I practiced and progressed, I started to pick up precious extra seconds. Thirty seconds turned into a minute, then a minute turned into a minute and a half. Then one day, holding my breath, I actually made it over the two-minute mark. My confidence grew and the torture cell started to look more and more like I could "own" it in my upcoming performance.

I knew that I could do it. Don't ask me how I knew I could do it, but I did. I had worked with Brett and helped stage it during his show when he escaped from it. I had been personally coached (by phone, nonetheless!) by Brett in the finer points of the escape. I could hold my breath for at least two minutes (on a good day.) Although I had never actually rehearsed the escape the way that I would actually be performing it (!), I knew that I could do it.

Oh yeah, about that...because my parent's garage was a normal garage, rehearsals were absolutely nothing like what an actual performance was going to be like. The best I could do was try to simulate what it would be like for real. In reality, my rehearsals were a far cry from an actual performance.

When I rehearsed with Aarron and Fred, Aarron would position a ladder next to the cell for me to climb. I would climb up the ladder and, in a makeshift "dive," I would enter the cell head first. Once I was fully immersed with my head at the bottom of the cell and my legs sticking out of the top, Aarron would hold my legs in place while he and Fred put the top on and locked my legs into the stocks so that I couldn't move. And after all of that, finally I could practice the escape. To an outsider, I probably would have looked like a complete nut, or like I was on my way to a watery grave in front of a live audience.

The simple truth is that, when I attempted to escape for real on Halloween, I wouldn't be dealing with any of that craziness. I would just be lowered into the cell head-first by a chain motor hung from the ceiling of the mall. But for now, this was my reality.

About three days before the date for the Houdini Challenge, Aarron, Fred, and I were in my parent's garage and I had just dived into the cell. As Aarron and Fred locked my legs into the stocks, I repositioned my head and a small amount of water got into my nose and forced me to cough. Here's a tip for you: try not to cough when you are being held upside-down underwater.

That cough made me swallow a large gulp of water and start to choke. I naturally started to fight with Aarron and Fred as they started to lock me into the leg stocks. Fortunately, I worked my way out of the cell without any further incident. But to add insult to injury, my Dad pulled his car into the other side of the garage right as this incident happened.

So, here is what my Dad saw: his son, submerged upside-down in a water torture cell, fighting to get free from two of his buddies who are holding him in place. And once his son got free of the cell, he was coughing and hacking like his buddies had just tried to drown him.

As I looked up and saw my Dad staring at me, I choked out the words, "I'm fine. I'm fine." He just shook his head and said, "That's great, Jason…just great." I'm sure it was just another strange incident in his mind with his slightly nutty entertainer son.

The weeks leading up to the Houdini Challenge were full of make-shift rehearsals in my parent's garage with Aaron and Fred, time spent at the YMCA pool, and sending out press releases. I was trying frantically to connect with local news outlets and schedule personal appearances on local television so I could capture that all-important TV footage for my promotional reel.

But no matter how much preparation Aarron, Fred, and I had, no matter how many laps I swam in the YMCA pool, no matter how long I could hold my breath, nothing could fully prepare us for the challenges we would face the day of the event.

CHAPTER TEN

I WOKE UP AT 3 a.m. Halloween morning ready to take on "The Houdini Challenge." I knew that I had to take hot water with me to counteract the cold water that I would initially fill the tank with when I arrived at the mall.

I already had several coolers filled with hot water that I had boiled the night before, but I spent the first few hours of the early morning boiling more water and packing it in the truck to take along.

Aarron, Fred, and I arrived at the mall around 6:30 a.m., to load the equipment in and meet with the mall event team.

My friend John and I had pitched the idea to the decision makers at the mall based on our good reputations, but these folks had never actually seen a performance. (For that matter, no one had ever seen me perform this thing, since I never actually had!) The mall event folks wanted to make sure I wasn't going to drown myself in the middle of their mall in front of a bunch of their guests.

We spent the next hour filling the Torture Cell with water from a hose, then trying to balance out the temperature with the hot water that I had packed ahead of time. While Aarron and Fred made sure the cell was full of water, I worked with the mall engineers to hang the chain motor that I had borrowed from Brett.

Although very few people realized it, the chain motor was an integral part of performing the escape. It is how I would be raised up and lowered into the cell upside down.

In our initial conversation, Brett pointed out to me that his chain motor was specially constructed to lower faster than most chain motors. The reason it had to lower more quickly was I wouldn't be able to breathe the moment my head went underwater. And I also wouldn't be able to start escaping from the cell until I was fully lowered and locked in place. So, the entire time that my body was being lowered, positioned, and locked into place was just dead time when I had to hold my breath and wait.

After the mall's engineers got the chain motor hung and the power run to it, the time arrived for me to escape from Houdini's Water Torture Cell for the mall staff.

Now here's the thing... everything that I had been working on for the last month hinged on a successful performance. Even though Aarron, Fred, and I had never actually run through this thing fully, we had to do it perfectly or the mall staff would scrap this whole event. No pressure!

Let me stop right here. If you are a magician or an entertainer considering a stunt or escape that is potentially life-threatening, do <u>not</u> follow my example. I repeat…do <u>not</u> do what I did. The chances of everything working out successfully for you are not good. In fact, if you are reading these words and are considering doing something even remotely dangerous, either…do not do it, or hire a professional team of consultants who can help you stage and execute it safely.

With that said, it's not like I didn't have experience staging this escape and executing it. Yes, it is true that I had never escaped from it in a situation quite like this, and yes, it is true that my team of Aarron and Fred had never done it either, but I did have experience with Brett. I also had a last-ditch escape plan just in case the escape failed. A sledgehammer.

Aarron, Fred, and I huddled together and reviewed each person's job. Aarron would lower the top stocks down to the ground. Fred and Aarron would then lock my legs into the stocks. Aarron then would raise the stocks, and me, into the air while Fred steadied me so that my body didn't swing around too much. Once I was in my position hanging high in the air, Fred would move the Torture Cell directly under me so that Aarron could lower me straight in. When I was fully submerged, the top stocks would be locked onto the top of the cell. And finally, Aarron and Fred would raise a curtain around the cell so that I could start my escape.

The only thing I had to do was escape a set of handcuffs while hanging upside down underwater and then find a way to pick the locks that held the top on. By the way, the locks were locked onto the outside of the cell while I was trapped on the inside of the cell. So basically, it boiled down to this… escape the handcuffs and locks, and escape a watery grave before I ran out of oxygen.

Tension filled the air. I knew that Aarron and Fred were tense since this was the first time they were doing their jobs from start to finish. The mall staff was tense because all of the talking and planning we had worked on together was now very real and very dangerous right in front of them. And I was tense because I knew we had to get this right in order to be cleared to perform this stunt that night in front of a busy mall.

Aarron lowered the stocks to the floor. Aarron and Fred locked my legs into the stocks. Aarron successfully raised me in the air and Fred moved the cell into position. Then I took several deep breaths, calmed myself, and gave Aarron the signal to lower me into the water.

When you are fully submerged upside-down in a tank of water, you almost lose some of your senses. You can't hear very much that is happening around you. It also becomes more difficult to see what is going on outside the cell even though the outside is only a foot away.

Once I dropped into the cell, my only job was to relax and wait until the guys got the top of the cell locked onto the Torture Cell. I would know that it was time to start my escape the moment that I saw the curtain raised around the cell.

You know, it's a little strange to say that when I was immersed and my senses were dulled by the water, it was a little bit calming. I didn't feel the tension that I know everyone watching from the outside of the cell felt. I was completely focused on the tasks I had to do while in the cell. Fortunately, my resolve wasn't tested because Aarron and Fred got me lowered into the cell and the top secured quickly.

I had probably been underwater for about twenty-five seconds when I saw the curtain go up around the cell to shield everyone's eyes from exactly how I was going to make my escape. The curtain's main job was to add a bit of mystery and suspense to what I was doing. Of course, it also added a bit of danger. While it did keep anyone watching from seeing exactly how I was going to do what I had to do inside the cell, it also kept my team from making sure that I didn't accidentally have a problem and need to be pulled out early. Let's just say that it added more tension to an already tense situation.

Once that curtain went up, though, I knew what I had to do and I set about doing it. The handcuffs didn't pose too much of a problem because I had been able to practice with them anytime I felt like it. It took me about thirty to forty seconds to escape from the cuffs.

Now I was faced with the hard part. Escape from the locks that held the top stocks onto the cell, even though the locks were on the outside of the cell and I was still upside down on the inside of the cell. Fortunately, I had developed a technique for this. And that technique had been tested and practiced during rehearsals in my parent's garage.

By this point in the escape, my team and I had successfully done everything right. The only thing holding us back from staging this stunt that night was this final part of the escape.

Performing the actual escape ended up being far more stressful than simulating the escape like we had been doing for the last several weeks. And while I relaxed myself as much as possible before the escape, I was definitely dealing with a more difficult situation. Because of the added stress of the situation, I started to have difficulty holding my breath. I knew that I could hold out for another thirty seconds, but anything more would be problematic.

But just like everything else that morning, the final part of the escape went exactly to plan. It took me about thirty to forty seconds to successfully execute the last part of the escape and I successfully emerged from the cell to the delight of the mall staff.

High fives and smiles greeted me from Aarron, Fred, and the mall staff as I caught my breath. We then went over final details with the mall's marketing team and finally got the green light for our performance that night.

We had done it. All the preparation, practice, and visualization had paid off. We had successfully staged my first escape from Houdini's Water Torture Cell under fire. And as happy as I was about our success that morning, in the back of my mind I secretly wondered if my next attempt at escaping the cell, in front of hundreds of people in the busy mall, would go as flawlessly as this one had. We would soon find out.

CHAPTER ELEVEN

M Y PHONE RANG right after lunch, a local Nashville number, but not one I recognized. On the other end of the line was a producer from the evening news at WSMV, the local NBC affiliate. The producer told me that one of their reporters, James Lewis, planned on doing live coverage of the Houdini Challenge that night.

That was a massive success for me. It meant that all the time crafting news releases and making phone calls trying to get the attention of the press had paid off. The Houdini Challenge would be one of the main news stories in Nashville and the middle Tennessee area on Halloween!

As I spoke to the producer, he asked me what time the event would begin. I told him the escape would take place a few minutes after 6 p.m., right in the middle of that evening's news broadcast.

I had scheduled it at that time on the remote chance that, maybe, I might get a news crew to come out and shoot the event for the 10 o'clock news. The producer excitedly told me that James would arrive at the mall several hours early to do an interview with me for several teaser segments that would air during the afternoon leading up to the 6 o'clock news. The producer also told me they might even get a live shot of some of the event during the news broadcast itself.

When I heard that, I knew exactly what I had to do. I had to stage the escape from the Torture Cell at the exact time that the evening news cut live to James Lewis at Opry Mills Mall. I knew, beyond a shadow of a doubt, that if I could time this whole thing so that I was in the middle of performing this death-defying feat that WSMV wouldn't be able to cut away to a commercial or to another story. I knew the station would have to stay with the live shot to show the viewers at home whether I drowned in front of a huge crowd at Opry Mills Mall or escaped from Houdini's Water Torture Cell alive.

James and his camera guy showed up around 4 p.m. I had been going over details with Aarron and Fred and working on last-minute adjustments. We were only two hours away from the start of the Houdini Challenge and the supporting cast for the evening had arrived.

James and I did an interview scheduled to run during the 5 o'clock news and I made sure to introduce my assistant, Monica, to James to show him and his viewers what the Torture Cell looked like up-close and personal.

As James and I were talking about the escape, I mentioned that, should I fail, my only way out would be with the sledgehammer that Monica held as she stood next to the cell. My gut instinct told me that this type of showmanship would guarantee excellent coverage of the escape just an hour later. And my gut instinct proved correct, as I would soon find out.

After the interview, James asked me what time I planned on escaping from the cell. I asked him what time would be best for the broadcast. After checking with his producers, we set a time. Everything was going to plan. I was optimistic that if we started the escape from the cell on time, I might get some of the event covered live.

As the clock ticked down closer and closer to 6 p.m., I continued working with my team. John, who had helped me sell this idea to the mall, arrived. My master of ceremonies and creative brainstorming partner, Nelson, arrived. Aarron and Fred drained out some of the cold water and leveled out the temperature of the cell by adding more hot water. Monica stood next to the cell with the sledgehammer making the stunt look potentially disastrous. And people arrived and arrived and arrived.

In some of his memoirs, Houdini wrote that, when someone threatened to put their life on the line to defy death, people would come out to see what happened. And that is exactly what transpired. After the two spots with James ran on the earlier news segments, the word got out and the public wanted to see the spectacle.

Opry Mills Mall has a beautiful circular stage in an area of the mall that can hold several hundred spectators. Being in Nashville, they usually used the stage to feature musicians. But tonight, at least at Opry Mills, Music City gave way to Magic City. As the last few minutes ticked away to 6 p.m., the start time of "The Houdini Challenge" event, the area around the circular stage became packed, with people as far as the eye could see.

As the clock struck 6 p.m., Nelson, my master of ceremonies, welcomed the crowd to the event. I had three different pieces to perform that evening inspired by Houdini: a performance of Houdini's famous Metamorphosis illusion, the needle-swallowing (which Houdini claimed he carried with him at all times in case of a last-minute, impromptu performance), and the Water Torture Cell.

We designed the entire event to take about half an hour with plenty of time built in between the performances to hype the featured escape. I opened the event with a performance of Houdini's Metamorphosis illusion.

Metamorphosis is visually impressive and surprising. You must watch every move closely or you'll miss the moment of magic, when it happens. I knew that performing Metamorphosis first would establish me as someone to watch closely and the event as one sure to deliver on all the hype.

The moment that my assistant Monica vanished and I visually appeared in her place there was a huge surge of energy in the room. This crowd was excited about what we were doing and they were ready for the magic.

After I finished Metamorphosis, I checked in with Aarron and Fred while Nelson continued to hype the escape from the Water Torture Cell. The guys told me that everything was ready. I found James and told him the exact time we would have me hanging upside-down by my ankles, poised above the cell, ready to be dropped in, so that he could be as prepared as possible.

I made my way back to the stage and focused everyone's attention on a very small, but stunning illusion – the needle-swallowing. Technically, the needle-swallowing uses very small items. However, when staged correctly with the right lighting, an audience can be enthralled with the action taking place. I was swallowing needles, swallowing a thread, and then regurgitating them with the needles threaded one by one onto the thread. My performance drew gasps from the crowd.

And then suddenly, as the echoes from the applause rang in my ears, the time arrived. All of the preparation and planning came to a head. I immediately had to get out of my entertainer's mind and enter into my survivor's mind. I knew that it would be easy for all the excitement of the event to sabotage my escape and I made a conscious decision to ignore everyone gathered and focus, solely, on what I had to do, step by step, over the next five minutes.

Nelson made a few last-minute remarks as we checked our watches to make sure we were going to have me in position at the agreed start time, so the news station could cut to a live shot of the escape in action.

I took off my show clothes to reveal a pair of swim trunks underneath my pants and a form fitting fitness shirt underneath my show shirt. I then laid down on the ground and offered up my legs to be locked into the leg stocks. After Aarron and Fred secured my legs into the stocks, they slowly raised me into the air by my ankles.

At this point, the rock music was blaring as I totally focused on the task at hand. As I hung upside-down, I watched my guys position the water torture cell directly beneath me. Aarron manned the chain motor control and Fred stood by, ready to steady the top stocks as they were about to be attached to the cell.

Aarron lowered me about a foot so that my head hung just barely above the cell and I could grab the top of the cell and steady myself. I took several deep breaths to calm and focus myself on the task at hand. Then I heard the music get to the rolling guitar solo and it was time.

I gave Aarron the signal to lower me into the water and within seconds I was submerged head first into what could potentially be a watery grave. I've heard people say that time slows down when faced with death. I certainly didn't feel like I was about to die, but I did know that this escape wasn't to be taken lightly.

The first thing I focused on was waiting. I waited to be sure that Fred and Aarron secured the ankle stocks onto the top of the cell. Then they raised a curtain around the torture cell so that the audience couldn't see what I was doing inside.

One of the main reasons for not wanting the audience to be able to see into the cell was so they wouldn't learn any specific secrets about how I executed my escape. The art of magic has taught me that some secrets are meant to be kept.

If I had escaped from the cell in full view of everyone, they would have learned secrets that took me years to acquire and a great deal of training to execute. Besides, magic tricks, illusions, and escapes are much more fun when an air of mystery surrounds them.

Raising a curtain around the cell as I started my escape also built tension. The name of the game, after all, is entertainment. Building tension and making the audience wonder just what I was doing added to the fun and excitement of the event.

I knew, based on my performance for the mall staff early that morning, that when the curtain went up, I plunged into, more or less, a sensory-deprivation chamber. As I was submerged, the water made me extremely lightweight, and took away (mostly) my ability to hear what was happening outside of the tank. When the curtain went up, there was nothing for me to see. Left with my own thoughts, I found it peaceful, but knew it also posed great danger.

After spending a few seconds in stillness, I started to make my escape. Because of all the time spent preparing, visualizing, and rehearsing, the escape itself went relatively straight forward. I didn't run into any major snags. I didn't have a near-death experience. I kept my calm, focused on each of the small steps to be completed, and did what had to be done.

The way we had staged the Water Torture Cell allowed me to escape a few seconds before the audience realized that I had escaped. As I hoisted myself out of the water and onto the top of the cell I felt an incredible thrill.

The entire process of escaping from the cell had taken several minutes, and throughout the escape, we constantly teased the audience by letting them see me for twenty or thirty seconds then obscuring their vision of what I was doing for a while. The tension in the mall must have been thick, because when Aarron and Fred lowered the curtain the final time to show that I had successfully escaped a watery grave, the mall erupted in cheering, yelling, and applause.

I had done it! I had successfully escaped from Houdini's Water Torture Cell in front of a live audience of almost a thousand people and a television audience of no telling how many tens or hundreds of thousands. And, in so doing, I had done the impossible. I had flirted with death and lived to tell about it.

Escaping from Houdini's Water Torture Cell put me on the map. With all the touring and production experience that I had learned from Brett Daniels in China, I knew that I could stage and execute a fantastic show in virtually any setting. And I finally felt like I had established myself as a force to be reckoned with.

I had recorded the live news footage at home and hit the jackpot. If I had hired a professional video production team to come and record the show, I couldn't have gotten a better outcome than I did with the news footage. Later that night, as I watched the recording, the evening news anchor introduced the piece and then the shot cut to me hanging upside down by my ankles just inches above the cell.

And to top it all off, the news channel stayed with the shot for almost three minutes. After all, they couldn't exactly cut away once I got lowered into the water. Everyone at home wanted to know what happened, providing some riveting television.

The Water Torture Cell helped me continue to promote my theatre shows around the area and build up my press kit. And I was riding high from that event for quite some time. But, as always, I soon realized that I needed to do something else to keep me in front of the public. My big question was: what can I do that would be bigger than a death-defying escape?

The answer would come soon enough.

****

To see the live news coverage of my escape from the Torture Cell, visit http://www.jasonmichaelsmagic.com/impossible-book

CHAPTER TWELVE

I WAS IN A very creative time in my career and my business. Since I had returned home from working with Brett in Tunica up until now, I had been spending a lot of time with a group of magic friends who performed together, pushed each other to work harder on our businesses, and who brainstormed interesting, creative ideas.

One day, as we worked on ideas at my friend John's house, I decided to "try out" something for the group. I had, what I thought, was an interesting idea. I had been working on creating some new, original material for my show and wanted to tackle the trick that magicians claim is what all great magicians can be measured by…the cups and balls.

I knew, based on my knowledge and research, that many magic historians believe the cups and balls trick to be thousands of years old, citing an historical cave drawing from Beni Hasan which dates to 2500 BCE.

My take on the piece was that I was going to perform the cups and balls trick as a Renaissance-era street performer. After all, I had been fascinated with Shakespeare since my theatre studies in college, and knew that taking a unique approach to this trick might grab a talent booker's attention, and that could open some more doors for me.

Even though I didn't really have a full-blown routine to show the group I wanted to get some initial feedback on the idea. So I took out my props, adopted what I thought was a decent English accent and started to play around with some moves and jokes in front of my friends. When I finished playing, the consensus was that I was on to something.

That feedback from my friends gave me a shot of confidence that I had an interesting idea that could lead to something special. I dove deeper into the idea and deeper into the Shakespearean-styled character. I had created many characters as an actor and even created characters for my magic show. But I had not committed this much effort to one of my magic routines.

As an actor, when you create a character, one of the important steps is to do a character analysis. A character analysis helps you get to know the person that you are creating and will play onstage. When doing a character analysis, I ask and answer all sorts of questions about this new person. The questions range from personal, family, and political background all the way to what dreams and goals this character has.

Doing a character analysis requires an in-depth process that allows an actor to create and learn as much about the character as possible. By doing this, the actor should be able to make choices on-stage that are congruent with the character. The goal is to make sure that all the choices made in front of an audience support who the character is in the audience's view, rather than conflict with who the audience believes this person to be.

As I worked on the character analysis, I spent a great deal of time imagining the character. And as I spent more and more time imagining "Francesco" in different situations, I began to "get to know" this lovable rogue. I asked myself questions about his background, his political leanings, and his family history and I relied heavily on my imagination to see, feel, and slowly become Francesco in my mind.

I also started to work on the "routine" — the moves of the actual trick itself. Because I used my imagination to "become" Francesco in my mind first, my physical choices and the decisions I made about the routine came easily. I embraced the comments, jokes, and sleights-of-hand that felt like Francesco would use, and dismissed the ones that didn't feel like choices he would make.

Fortunately, a regional magicians' conference was coming up soon and everyone from my brainstorming group planned on being there. In fact, we planned to make quite a splash, our goal being to have the main performers of the group enter the contests and take all the top prizes. We figured that would make quite an impression!

I focused all my attention on working on this one routine, my Shakespearean cups and balls. Over the next few months, I worked on and learned the sequence of moves that I thought made for a good routine. I purchased new props. I worked on defining and becoming the character in front of an audience.

I had a costume made. I spent a great deal of time in practice and rehearsal. I did everything necessary to prepare for the upcoming contests.

Because of the amount of practice and rehearsal I invested in this routine, there is no doubt that I was ready when the conference arrived. I planned on competing in the close-up competition with my new Cups and Balls routine, and I also planned on entering the stage competition with another new piece. Since I had never competed in a contest before, you might say I was a little ambitious, but very confident. What else was new!

The conference was a blast. There were magicians hanging out everywhere and we all enjoyed making new friends and trying to make our mark on the local magic community.

The morning of the contests I arrived at the conference early. I had been spending a huge amount of time rehearsing both of my acts and imagining the contest scenario, and I was ready.

After attending a contest meeting, I found myself waiting in the hallway outside of the close-up contest room. There were quite a few contestants vying for the prize and I was up next. I heard the audience applaud as the performer before me took their final bow and suddenly it was time.

The contest chairman introduced me and I took the room by storm. I had made the very specific choice of not setting up anything in front of the audience. Because I had all the necessary props on my person, I was able to wait until after my introduction to burst into the room and grab everyone's attention.

My entrance was very different from the way that all the other magicians started their contest acts because I looked at the situation through the lens of an actor. As an actor, you become the character before you take the stage and step in

One of my performances of my Cups and Balls routine.

front of an audience. All I did was choose to become the character before I walked into the room, something that actors do all of the time, but was a new idea for a magician to do. The moment that I walked through the door, I was playing a larger-than-life, lovable-rogue street performer.

Because I entered the room with a larger-than-life amount of energy, I carried that level of energy throughout the entire act. It was great fun to poke fun at the audience as I played the role. All the techniques and sequences went flawlessly and the audience rewarded me with enthusiastic applause.

That evening, during the final stage show, the contest winners were announced. And while I wasn't totally surprised, I was extremely excited when my name was called in first place in the close-up magic category.

One of the coolest things that happened to me at the competition, besides winning first place, was for several well-established magicians to pull me aside and compliment me. In addition to being very kind with their comments, they also wanted to give me some ideas on how I could improve my act so that I could compete at the international level.

I was very appreciative of their comments and ideas. In fact, several of their ideas inspired me to rework some of the sequences to create a more impactful, visual act. One that would, no doubt, have a better chance of winning a place later that year at the international conferences.

That was the long-term goal, after all. Winning an international competition would put me in front of all sorts of international buyers and booking agents.

I got back to work over the next several months, reworking the routine, defining my character even more, with lots of rehearsal and performing. Every time I had a show, I included my cups and balls routine. I wanted to have so much time and energy invested in my competition act that I could perform it flawlessly under any circumstances. My dedication to that goal proved to be pivotal.

In the summer of 2005, the International Brotherhood of Magicians (IBM) annual convention was held in Reno, Nevada, and the Society of American Magicians (SAM) annual conference followed in Boston. The two conventions each had their own competition, with the two events only a week apart.

I was super excited to have most of the guys from my brainstorming group also attending the IBM convention in Reno. In fact, my friend John also entered the competition!

The IBM competition was quite a bit larger than the local and regional competitions that I had competed in up until this point. At the contest meeting, there were dozens of competitors and I learned that the competition extended over two days with a preliminary round followed by a final round.

In the preliminary round, each competitor had to perform in four different rooms for four different audiences. The judges spread out over the rooms, tasked with evaluating the artistic, performance, and technical merits of each performer.

All the competitors (between 35 and 40) gathered in a large holding room that was quite a sight. Some magicians talked to each other, others went through some last-minute practicing, and a few were trying desperately to psych out all of their competition.

Finally, the announcer called my name and I headed to the first room and reported to the room monitor. I waited in the large hallway as the competitor before me did his act. Then I was on.

In a sense, it was very similar to my first competition. When the room monitor announced my name, I took the room by storm ringing the bell that started my act. I used this same approach in each of the four rooms that I performed in that morning.

After that morning's preliminary round, I saw my friends standing in the hallway. I wanted to get their feedback. They told me that I was one of the highlights of competition and they thought I had a very strong chance of making it into the finals round.

That evening, in the main showroom, I gave high fives and fist bumps to my friends when they announced my name along with six others to advance to the finals two days later.

The finals round was similar to the preliminary rounds, with multiple performances in multiple rooms in front of multiple judges. Each room that I performed in had a big turnout, since all the convention attendees wanted to see the performers who were good enough to get passed on to this round. I performed my act and felt good about it.

That night, at the final stage show, all the contest winners were announced. As the contest chairman took the microphone, the room went silent. The first few awards were given out and then came time to announce the winners of the close-up competition. Slightly apprehensive, I was a little relieved when third place was announced and it wasn't me. I hoped that meant that I was in the final two.

A few seconds later the announcer said, "And coming in second place, from Nashville TN...Jason Michaels!" I had done it! I had taken second place in the close-up competition of the International Brotherhood of Magicians big convention.

First place was taken by a gentleman named Ivan Amodei, the one guy all of my friends told me would probably be my biggest competition.

I was pretty dang excited! Less than a year before, I had decided to start entering magic competitions as a way to get my name out into the community, and now I had taken second place among a group of competitors from all over the world.

The only thing left for me to do was to go to Boston the following week and try to win the Society of American Magicians international competition at their annual convention. If only it were that easy!

I flew home triumphant, officially an award-winning magician on an international level. I spent the next couple of days continuing to rehearse my act and make sure that it was the best it could possibly be.

I left Nashville for Boston the afternoon before the convention was set to start. As I sat in the Nashville airport, I learned that my flight was delayed. Flight delays are always the pits. But they are even more frustrating when you are on a timeline and must be at a specific place by a specific time.

When we finally took off, I knew we would be cutting it close to catch my connecting flight to Boston. As we got close to our connecting airport, we started to make circles. I didn't know why we weren't coming in to land, but I did know that the more we circled, the less chance I had to make my next flight.

When we finally did land and I got into the airport, I found out that the flight I had to catch had left without me. To make matters worse, when I went to the service desk I was told that the next flight out was the next morning at 6 a.m. And to add insult to injury, the attendant told me the airline would not be paying for a hotel room for me for the night!

I was ticked! I was so ticked off that I absolutely refused to go to a hotel and pay for a room solely on principle. I felt like the airline didn't get me where I was supposed to go and that they should pay for my room. Since they weren't going to pay for my room, then to heck with 'em...I'll just stay at the airport and get more and more ticked off!

Just for the record, I don't recommend trying to sleep in an airport the day before you have a very important event – like an international magic competition. In fact, I barely slept at all.

The next morning, I boarded the airplane and flew to Boston. I arrived, gathered my bags, and took a taxi to the hotel hosting the convention.

I gave the lady my name to check in at the front desk and she told me the hotel didn't have a reservation for me. I was confused. Because I barely slept the night before, I felt like I was in a fog. I told her that I originally was supposed to come in the day before and that I had missed my connecting flight, thinking that maybe that was why she couldn't find my reservation.

She still couldn't find my reservation. I realized that I had a choice. I could choose to be a victim... after all, I had been treated poorly by the airline after their failure to provide the service they had contracted with me, or, I could choose to be a victor and deal with this situation the best that I possibly could.

I took a deep breath and then I realized something very simple through the haze fogging my mind. Perhaps they still had rooms available. I told the young lady that I didn't know why they didn't have my reservation, but that I was attending the big magic convention and hoped to stay there with everyone else.

A few minutes later, I felt the stress drain out of my shoulders, back, and arms as I fell backwards into the very soft bed in the room that the front desk attendant booked me into. Exhausted and still quite a bit stressed from the last twenty-four hours, I set the alarm and fell asleep for a couple of hours before the contest started.

I woke up from a deep sleep with enough time to take a shower, stretch out, and run through my act one or two times before the competition began.

The SAM competition was structured differently from the IBM competition. At the SAM competition, I had already submitted a video of my full act to be reviewed by a contest panel before being selected to go straight into the finals round.

Not having to perform in a preliminary round was both a blessing and a curse. The blessing was not having to perform a bunch of extra times in order to make it into the finals. You never know when something might go wrong in a live performance and hurt your chances of winning.

The curse was that my first performances would be in totally unfamiliar spaces I would be seeing for the first time. Believe it or not, seeing the performance space and getting comfortable in it is very important for most performers.

So here I was again…standing outside a hotel meeting room waiting for another magician to finish their act so that I could be introduced and give it my best shot.

At this contest, I performed my cups and balls act in three different rooms over the course of an hour and a half. And after it was all said and done, I was pretty happy. I had flown in early in the morning after a night of almost no sleep, checked into a hotel that I didn't think had a place for me to stay, caught up on enough sleep to help me focus, and then successfully performed in an unbelievably stressful situation as knowledgeable magicians and judges watched with a critical eye – an international competition.

The next two days of the convention were just fun. The competition was one of the first things of the convention and now I could just kick back and attend fun lectures and shows as I waited for the big announcements scheduled for the final day.

I was sitting in the showroom the final day of the conference as the contest chairman took the microphone to announce the contest winners. I really didn't have a clue if I would do well in this contest or not. I had been fortunate to have guys from my mastermind crew at all my other competitions so I could grill them for details of what the other performers did. At this convention, though, I was alone.

The first few announcements awarded different superlative awards such as for outstanding creativity, the award for comedy, and one for inventions. Then my category arrived. Third place was announced first and my name was not called. Now I was nervous. I either did really well, or I was outclassed and outperformed by the other contestants.

"The second-place award goes to, from Nashville, TN, Jason Michaels!" the loudspeakers boomed.

I smiled both on the inside and on the outside. I had taken second place…again! Well, at least I was consistent. I knew my act was pretty darn good to win second place at both major conventions.

"And first place goes to, from California, Ivan Amodei!"

I couldn't believe it. The same guy beat me at both the IBM and the SAM competitions! I guess he was consistent too.

I flew home the next morning with another second-place trophy and, more importantly, a new level of confidence.

In less than a year, I had gone from a relatively new magician on the magic scene, scrapping and hustling to create opportunities for work and ways to get paid, to an internationally award-winning magician.

My gut instinct had been right. I had deeply believed, way down in my gut, that I was good enough as a performer and magician to compete with and perform with some of the best magicians on the planet. The awards that I had amassed over the last year had validated and confirmed that. Now it was time to make all those awards pay off.

✱✱✱

To see my Cups and Balls competition act, visit http://www.jasonmichaelsmagic.com/impossible-book

CHAPTER THIRTEEN

The next several years were full of interesting opportunities. While I'm not sure I can directly attribute the awards I won to specific bookings or contracts, I am positive that my level of confidence to sell my show and perform in all sorts of unique settings came from those competitions and those awards.

I pursued working the college market on a full-time basis and found myself travelling all over the country to different campuses to perform my show.

I worked with Brett Daniels again several times with his show when I had slow periods in my own business.

I thoroughly enjoyed working on cruise ships performing my show on a regular basis.

I opened my business to providing entertainment for corporate groups at sales meetings, conferences, trade shows, and at VIP events.

I was having some good success. What was interesting though, was that the tics with my Tourette's Syndrome had started to come back.

It had been quite a while since I had been on any sort of medication. After all, my doctors told me that as I got older the tics would fade away. I honestly couldn't remember the last time I had taken any sort of medication, but as I got into my thirties the uncontrollable, sudden, repetitive movements started to make life almost unbearable again.

I was twitching and making strange movements so frequently and so intensely that I reached out to Vanderbilt University Medical Center in the hopes of finding a specialist who could help put a stop to the insanity.

Right before my first appointment with a neurosurgeon, I heard about a procedure where a surgeon implants an electrode into your brain designed to stimulate the part of the brain associated with Parkinson's Disease and other movement disorders. This procedure, called Deep Brain Stimulation, had been tried on several patients with severe cases of Tourette's Syndrome with good results.

I wasn't sure that I wanted to have an electrode surgically inserted into my brain, but I knew I wanted those damn tics to stop and I considered it.

The decision seemed to be made for me though, because when I met with the neurosurgeon, he told me that he didn't think I had a severe enough case to warrant a procedure still very new which didn't guarantee the results I sought.

I did, however, get a referral to a neurologist at Vanderbilt who was very knowledgeable on Tourette's Syndrome and other, related disorders.

A very calm, very nice man, Neurologist Dr. Michael Cooper speaks softly and listens to everything you tell him. He has caring eyes and a warm smile and I saw him several weeks later.

I'm almost always very uncomfortable when I am at a doctor's office for treatment of Tourette's. This visit began the same way. I just hate feeling like I'm constantly being observed and watched while some doctor tries to determine the level of severity of my tics during the extremely short period that he or she spends in my presence.

However, Dr. Cooper had a very kind bedside manner and made me feel comfortable when I spoke with him about the frustrating tics that had recently come back into my life. At the end of the appointment, he gave me a prescription for a medication that actually did reduce the severity of the tics.

As I stayed busy with shows at colleges, on cruise ships, and at corporate events, my friend, Stephen Bargatze, asked me if I would fill in for him from time to time at some of his speaking events.

Stephen, in addition to being one of the world's finest comedy magicians, also speaks regularly to young people about his personal story of overcoming an extremely difficult childhood, full of impossible-to-overcome obstacles, to become a world champion magician and comedian.

I told Stephen, in very specific terms, that I would be happy to fill in for him at his events and perform magic and speak on the topic of bullying, but I had zero interest in talking about Tourette's Syndrome. I had no interest in pointing out something that I viewed as my weakness.

A rope trick from one of my shows.   Photo by Rick Malkin

You see, for years I had wanted to be a superman on stage. I wanted to step onto the stage and be so amazing, so charming, and so cool that everyone in the audience would be in awe of me. The last thing I wanted to do was to walk onstage and then point out my flaws and weaknesses.

The whole point of competing in international competitions was to prove that I was an outstanding magician and excellent entertainer. I wanted the men in the audience to want to be like me and for the women in the audience to want to be with me. The last thing I wanted was for anyone in the audience to think about how good of a magician I was, especially since I had a disability.

It's already hard enough to step onstage for most people. Now Stephen wanted me to walk onstage and be completely vulnerable, to the point of feeling exposed and naked, with a bunch of strangers? Nope. Not going to happen.

Stephen said that talking about bullying and performing my show as his substitute from time to time would be great. So, I did. And then it happened. In a freak golf cart accident, Stephen broke his leg and wasn't able to perform or speak at any events for several months.

Over the next few months, I spoke in Stephen's place quite a few times. And while I didn't want to talk about having Tourette's, I did want to connect with the young people I spoke to. So, I started sharing thoughts about feeling different from everyone else. The more groups I spoke to, the more I shared what the embarrassment and shame felt like when someone made comments that alienated me.

That didn't translate into being more comfortable talking in depth about Tourette's, but if Stephen Bargatze is anything other than funny and a great magician, it's relentless. He knew I had been sharing about what it felt like to be different. Now he was on a mission.

Over the next several years, Stephen would mention, every now and then, about how I could incorporate my story of having Tourette's into my shows. Or he would have me substitute at another of his programs and would give me ideas on how I could tell more about having Tourette's during the message portion of the show.

I don't know this for a fact, but I honestly think he had me substitute for him at a few of his events just so I would be out there getting more and more comfortable sharing parts of my story with audiences.

Stephen could see something that I couldn't see. Because he had been giving his talk and telling his story for so long, he knew how his message touched people's hearts.

Stephen knew that every audience includes people who need to escape from the pain in their lives. For Stephen, that meant that he wanted to give them a few moments of laughter, fun, and amazement. And, for certain audiences, he knew he needed to get wide open and vulnerable with them, by telling his story so that the people who needed to hear his message of hope would hear it.

He also knew that being able to perform his comedy and magic was as much a gift for him as for his audiences. He wanted to pay back that gift over and over by helping to heal other people.

Part of the reason I love entertaining people is to give them those few moments of fun and amazement. I love to share a unique and special experience with them. I believe that inspiring people and helping them escape from their troubles and worries is a very noble thing.

But until I stood on the side of the stage watching Stephen tell his story to an audience of young people one day, I didn't know just how powerful, profound, and needed more stories like his could be.

In my quest to become a superman on stage, I had been blind and too proud to see the opportunity gifted to me.

I was talented onstage. I had paid my dues and learned what worked and what didn't work every time I stepped in front of a group. I could speak and communicate well. I was a fine storyteller and an internationally award-winning magician. And yet, I was lacking.

Until that day, when I watched Stephen touch the hearts, minds, and souls of the young people in his audience, I didn't understand that it wasn't about me.

My whole performing career had been about me, and yet in that one moment of seeing young people tell Stephen about how he had just changed their lives by telling his story, it became clear to me that my talent would not be used to its fullest potential until I became willing to be honest and open with my audiences, too. I needed to put my ego aside and focus on how to truly bless the people in my audiences by sharing my most personal, sometimes painful struggles.

That day, I finally understood why Stephen had been so relentless in pushing me to talk about the struggles that I had faced in my life. Stephen knew, all too well, that everyone deals with struggles. Some are visible and obvious, others silent and invisible. No matter what the struggle, we all need to hear and understand that we don't struggle alone. We all struggle together and we need each other's support to survive and thrive.

That was a big day for me. That was the day I decided that, in addition to being an entertainer, I had to really become a speaker.

Acting had come naturally to me. I loved to play characters who said and did things onstage that I would never do in real life. And I approached magic like I approached acting — I created a character I could play, a metaphorical mask that I could wear, that appeared as a great magician and entertainer. It just wasn't that difficult for me to do.

Speaking about my struggles with Tourette's Syndrome, on the other hand, that was entirely different. I was scared as hell.

CHAPTER
FOURTEEN

M Y EYES WERE closed. I was taking slow, deep breaths in through my nose and out through my mouth. I'd escaped the dressing room where all the other speakers were sitting around talking and made my way down the hall and around a corner and I was sitting cross-legged against a wall meditating — trying to calm myself.

What was I thinking? And why in the world had I decided to give my first full, dedicated talk on having Tourette's Syndrome at a TEDx conference?

If I'm guilty of anything in my decision-making process, it is that it sometimes takes me a long time to fully internalize and convince myself that certain ideas and decisions are the right next steps for me. Some of my closest friends can see the obvious next steps and try to convince me to take them. But I have to fully wrap my head around the ideas, and sometimes that takes a while.

When I finally set my mind to something and make the decision to commit, however, I dive straight into the deep end.

It was that way with my decision to become a magician, to attempt escaping from the water torture cell, and now this – deciding to talk about my Tourette's Syndrome.

I had really done it this time. I had full confidence in my ability to step onto a stage. I knew that I could "kill" a performance in front of a group like this. But when I submitted my information to the selection committee, I hadn't considered that this wasn't a "performance" by an actor or magician. It was a talk – by and about me!

I hadn't been in very many situations where the butterflies in my stomach were fluttering around quite this strong. My nerves were on edge. I couldn't stop thinking about how this talk would be broadcast live on the internet and then edited and live online, probably for the rest of my life. I had to "kill" this talk. It was too important.

The talks I had given for my friend, Stephen, had been relatively brief and only after a thirty- to forty-minute magic show. In other words, I warmed up my audiences by entertaining them first, then shared parts of my story after all the laughter and amazement had won them over.

Now I had created a talk that didn't have any cover. I wasn't winning over my audience with magic first. I selected the magic I would do in the program specifically to illustrate my points and the story about my life. And I wasn't sharing small parts of my story. I was sharing all my frustrations, embarrassment, and pain.

For some reason, I had talked myself into thinking that an audience would actually want to hear about my struggles with overcoming my disorder. What in the heck was I thinking?!? The butterflies in my stomach kept flying strong.

When I originally submitted for the conference, I intended to share my story, which I had summarized as an inspirational message of overcoming challenges that appear to be impossible. As I prepared for the TEDx conference, though, I received guidelines that TED speakers are asked to try to follow.

While the guidelines did mention that an effective presentation can be crafted in many ways, they specifically recommended ideas that TED found effective. Some of their guidelines included introducing evidence that supported how and why my idea could be implemented. The guidelines also stated that the primary goal of my talk was to communicate an idea effectively, not to tell a story or evoke emotions. This was problematic.

I didn't feel like I had one main idea. I definitely didn't have evidence. And the whole point of my talk was to tell a story and evoke emotions. Well damn!

As I focused on creating my presentation leading up to the conference, I tried to find a balance of my story and a main theme, along with evidence that I could share. This lead to frustration initially, but I'm very happy that I pushed myself to follow the recommended guidelines and find my underlying theme.

So here I was… a few minutes from giving my talk, confident that I had crafted a good presentation. I had learned it and rehearsed it over and over in front of a mirror and several close friends.

Yes, I was nervous. There was no doubt about that. But I also felt prepared and that this was the right next step for me and taken with noble intent – to help heal other people's pain and inspire them to live bigger, bolder lives.

It's certainly true that sometimes I take an exorbitant amount of time to finally make a decision that some of my friends can easily see. Then again, when I finally do embrace that next step in my life, I do it with full understanding. By the time I get to "yes, I'm going to do this," I have completely internalized why and I stand behind my decision one hundred percent.

So that's what brought me to this spot with my back against the wall, taking deep breaths, relaxing myself, I knew that I stood in the exact right place at the exact right time making the exact right decision. And that helped me channel my nerves away from fear and into excitement. I was ready to step out in front of four or five hundred people, and the unforgiving lens of a live camera, to give my talk.

A few moments later, I stood right off the side of the stage, strapped firmly into a straitjacket, watching my introduction. I focused myself. The moment I was introduced I stepped out into the harsh spotlight and had the audience's rapt attention.

I had decided to take a big risk by opening my talk by describing what it was like to be a young boy who felt trapped inside his own body, while I simultaneously attempted to escape from an authentic straitjacket.

I knew this was a long way from a typical opening of a speech. But that is exactly why I did it. I wanted my audience to be jarred by the visual of me being strapped into a straitjacket and then to take the imaginary journey in their minds with me as I described what it had sometimes felt like growing up with the disorder.

The audience erupted in applause the moment I finally escaped from the straitjacket. My visual metaphor accomplished my intention — gaining full empathy from everyone watching and listening. They chose to go with me to that place in their minds and now were fully open to hearing the rest of the story. I dove right in.

I chose a straitjacket to open my TEDx talk.

I was slightly surprised when I came to the end of my talk. My story, the principles that I discussed, and the magic that I performed had flowed so naturally. I had done it. I had done something that only a few years before would have been impossible for me to do. I had overcome self-doubt and massive resistance and shared my story with the world.

****

To watch my TEDx talk "You Can Do the Impossible, Too," visit http://www.jasonmichaelsmagic.com/impossible-book

CHAPTER FIFTEEN

L IVE BIG! B-I-G. That was my message. That is what I wanted to share to inspire and motivate my audience. But what exactly did it mean? What was I trying to explain that day in Chattanooga, TN, that would help others see beyond the limitations that they place on themselves and live bigger, bolder lives than they ever thought possible?

Because of the suggested guidelines from the TED conference that I forced myself to follow for my talk, I identified several very specific principles I had learned in my life, concepts that had helped me accomplish the goals I set for myself. These were principles that I had found worked for me to overcome challenges that appeared to be impossible. These were the techniques that helped me challenge myself to succeed at a very high level.

Live BIG! The **B** is for **Belief**. The **I** for **Imagination**. And the **G** is for **Go Forth**. So how does this little formula work?

B - Belief is foundational. It is what makes us who we are. The things we believe about ourselves and the world around us shape our philosophy of the world, the way we talk to ourselves, and the relationships that we have with those around us, just to name a few of the things that belief influences.

When I decided to go out for the Junior/Senior play at my school, I did it because it sounded fun. Never in my mind did I think to myself, "Hey, that may not be such a good idea since you have an uncontrollable, movement disorder." Had I allowed that type of doubt to enter my mind, I probably wouldn't have taken the risk and decided to audition. And if I still had decided to audition, my self-talk – the words and thoughts in my mind about what I was doing — could have easily sabotaged the entire experience.

When I started working for Brett in Tunica, and the production manager told me that the guy I was supposed to learn everything from had just quit, I faced the daunting task of having to learn how to execute six or seven grand stage illusions, as well as how to ride a motorcycle, in less than a day. It would have been very easy to have been overwhelmed by such a daunting task. But instead of freaking out, I looked Peter right in the eyes and told him that everything would be just fine because I could do it.

I told him that because I fully believed it. In my mind, I was perfect for the job and I wanted to prove that Brett had just hired an all-star. The simple truth was that I didn't have any experience with any of this large equipment. I'd never been on a motorcycle a day in my life, especially not one as big as the one I had to learn how to ride.

Had I allowed myself to entertain the idea that I probably wouldn't be able to learn it all in such a short period of time, then I'm sure I wouldn't have been able to. The fact that I believed that I could do it helped create the reality.

When my friend, Stephen, tried to convince me that I should start talking about growing up with and living with Tourette's Syndrome, I wouldn't even hear of it. I heard his argument. I heard what he told me, but I made it very clear that it wasn't going to happen.

I believed at the time that sharing my experiences with a neurological disorder would make me appear weak. I believed audiences wouldn't hold me to the high standard that I sought because they would feel sorry for me. I did not believe my story would inspire and touch other people's hearts. Because of my beliefs at the time, it was impossible for me to tell my story. I simply couldn't do it.

I had to change my beliefs; I had to change the story I was telling myself about having Tourette's Syndrome and how other people would view me before I could open my mind to the idea that I could help other people and be a source of inspiration, motivation, and success.

What I refer to as the "hyper-focus" that I developed as a child when I thought people's eyes were watching me has helped me believe that I can control the tics. Even if that control is very small and only lasts for a short time, that belief gives me extra confidence and helps me deal with the difficult days.

I haven't talked about my Christian faith in this book at all, but it is important to note that one of my foundational beliefs is that Jesus Christ is my Savior. I have a deep faith and rock-solid belief that God loves me as one of his most precious children.

I certainly don't understand why I have Tourette's Syndrome, but I know, deep in my soul, that God has always had, and always will have, my back. I know that when I am not strong enough, I can turn to Him and He will give me the strength I need to conquer every obstacle.

What I believe has shaped everything in my life. It has shaped who I am today, the things I have accomplished, the adventures I've had, and the way that I choose to live my life.

The big question is… what do you currently believe? Do you believe that you can live the life you've always dreamed of? Do you believe that you are a victim, or a conqueror? Do you see obstacles that are too big to overcome, or do you believe you can overcome any obstacle?

I hope you can see from the stories I have shared with you that what you believe is what you become.

I – Imagination is preparation for greatness. If you want to accomplish great things and become a high achiever in life, imagination is the next step.

When I committed to escaping from the Water Torture Cell, even though I had never escaped from it before, I used a huge amount of imagination. In my training, preparing my helpers, and the days of rehearsal leading up to the performance,

I ran through every step of the staging and the escape in my mind.

Part of the training of my technical assistants also forced them to use their imaginations. Because we didn't have any-where to stage a real rehearsal, I described to them what their jobs would entail and then we acted out what each of them had to do on the day of the event. We simulated everything in our minds and walked through the steps in our imaginations and in real life.

One of my imagination techniques is to see, in detail, from every point of view, the entire picture of what I'm going to do in my mind. I play a video in my mind of what it will look like when I accomplish whatever I am imagining.

Not only do I want to know what it will look like from my point of view, I also want to know what it will look like from an audience member's perspective. I want to know what it is going to look like from my technical assistant's points of view. I want to see it all in my mind's eye.

I then start to imagine what it is going to feel like to go through the process. Will I be nervous and need to calm myself? What will it feel like as I'm actually doing what needs to be done? How much pride will I feel the moment I accomplish what I set out to do?

I genuinely try to see in detail and feel the emotions I will feel at the time of accomplishment. This allows me to ampli-fy my imagination from simply daydreaming to a powerful visualization.

When I finally committed to speaking, I knew that it would be a challenge. The first thing I did was to change my belief. The second thing, after accepting the invitation to speak at the TEDx conference, was to start working on my talk.

Part of my process of writing and rewriting my talk was to rehearse it. When I rehearse a new creation, I talk through it as I see my audience in my mind's eye. In other words, I'll stand in front of a wall and deliver my presentation as I imagine a group of people watching me. I also imagine their response as I deliver a program. I imagine some audience members who are totally engaged and others who aren't. I genuinely try and feel the energy of the room.

By imagining, in detail, people watching and responding to what I'm doing onstage, I create a vivid scenario in my mind that truly prepares me. Focused imagination provides an incredibly powerful tool in my arsenal that has never let me down.

As I created my Cups and Balls competition act, I used my imagination vividly. I employed my imagination as I worked through the character analysis. I imagined what Francesco's clothing should look like if he were really performing at a Renaissance marketplace during Shakespeare's day. I practiced my script aloud to an empty room imagining an audience in front of me reacting to different jokes and sleight-of-hand sequences. I saw, in my mind, what each competition would be like before I ever set foot in any of the competition rooms.

When I started working for Brett, I spent a full day taking notes and paying very close attention to the guy who trained me. When it came time to start practicing and rehearsing each of the illusions I participated in, I basically knew what to do and when. One of the keys to my success was making sure I was very clear in my mind on what I had to do in each illusion to successfully execute it. I could practice my job in my imagination for hours, when it wasn't possible to practice it in person.

When I was rehearsing with the cast of the Junior/Senior play, I often imagined the theatre full of people. I would be saying my lines and interacting with the other actors onstage during rehearsal, while I pretended that there was a full audience watching me. That probably was one of the reasons that I wasn't nervous on the opening night of the play.

Seeing each of these situations in my imagination was like I had already lived them. By pretending to live them, when I stepped into a situation for the first time in real-life, my nerves were much calmer and I felt much more prepared than if I hadn't used my imagination techniques.

I know that you have used your imagination when you've read a book, or listened to someone tell a story, or remembered a wonderful time in your life. When was the last time you engaged your imagination, vividly, to see yourself accomplish something amazing in your life? It is a powerful tool. I hope you'll try it out and see the incredible results.

G – Go Forth. Go forth and take action. Go forth and do.

If belief opens your mind to new possibilities and opportunities, and imagination helps you see and feel yourself accomplishing the challenges that used to feel impossible, going forth and taking action, or doing as I like to put it, is where the rubber meets the road.

There is a popular joke that I like to cite in my speaking program that goes like this… How do you eat an elephant? One bite at a time.

I became an internationally award-winning magician by taking these steps. First, I believed I could create and perform a piece of magic that would stand out from the competition and win awards. Second, I used my imagination to see myself beating the competition and winning the awards. I also saw my audiences watching me in my imagination as I rehearsed and practiced. But most importantly, I took action.

My secret to taking action lies in doing it in steps. When I go forth and start taking action, I break down what actions must be taken into small, easy to accomplish steps. To start winning magic awards, some of my steps looked like this…

- Go through my repertoire and consider if any of my current magic routines would be a good starting point for a competition act.

- Make a list of tricks and ideas that I have liked over the years that excite me that would be a good starting point.

- Ask other magicians who have competed what it was like to compete and what the judges look for in a competition act.

- Try out some ideas in front of some trusted friends and listen to their feedback.

- Decide on a direction for the act and commit to it.

- Learn the technical handling for the routine/trick I plan to do.

- Write an initial script of what I will say in the act.

- Be open to playing around with the handling to see if I can come up with new ideas.

- Purchase any needed costumes.

- Purchase any needed props.

- Do an in-depth character analysis of my performance character.

- Commit to a certain amount of time to rehearse.

- Register for the conventions and competitions.

- Save money for any necessary travel.

- Et cetera, et cetera, et cetera.

That's not the entire list of what I did, but exemplifies how I broke down a lofty goal into easily accomplished steps.

Then I started checking things off the list. In other words, I started taking action every single day until I had accomplished what I set out to accomplish.

Do you have to write down every step you think it will take to accomplish your goal? No, of course not. The main idea is that you go forth and take action every single day. Some days, taking action may feel like a tiny step forward. Other days, it will feel like you've made a huge leap forward. The key to taking action is to take consistent steps every day that get you closer and closer to overcoming that challenge until you have done it.

Personally, I do write down what I'm focusing on accomplishing. Writing my outcome down on a piece of paper that I can review and focus on every day provides another one of my secret weapons. There's something amazing that happens in my mind when I take the time to write down what I plan to do. It's almost as if my intention goes from being a good idea to being something very concrete destined to happen.

One of my favorite things to do as I go through the process of step-by-step action is to cross through my list. As I take a step forward, I love to cross through that action item upon completion. Then, when I have difficult days where I am going up against mental resistance, I can look at all the items I have crossed off my list on my way to conquering and overcoming my impossible challenge.

If I'm being completely honest, I must tell you this... changing your mindset and imagining yourself overcoming your challenges gets you nowhere if you don't actually take action.

In fact, if you want to get really ticked off and disillusioned, just sit around for days on end and think about how amazing it will be to overcome your biggest challenge but don't do anything. You'll get seriously ticked off. You'll be ticked off at me, at yourself, and at the world. And why is that?

It's because when you change your beliefs, and start to imagine yourself doing great things, your mind and your body start preparing for action. By not taking action, you aren't acting congruently with your new beliefs. That causes massive frustration.

The biggest hurdle with taking action is thinking about it. Many times, when we think we are ready to take action, we start to imagine negative scenarios that might happen when we take the first few steps.

I knew that I was about to begin an amazing adventure when I got hired to work for Brett Daniels in Tunica, MS. I was so sure that this was a once-in-a-lifetime opportunity that I didn't even consider what bad things could happen.

When I drove away from Nashville, TN, that Sunday morning, I didn't even know where I would stay that night! But I did know that I was going to follow my show business dreams. By not entertaining negative self-talk, I opened myself up to a brand-new, exciting chapter in my life.

With that said, I can't count how many times that I've been ready to take action on a new project and then started to think about all the negative things that could happen if I started moving forward.

In those instances, I imagined taking action with my old mindset. Those negative scenarios didn't even exist. They were me making up things based on the way that I used to think. When my mindset focused on thoughts that I couldn't possibly overcome a challenge or accomplish a major goal, thinking about taking action was almost paralyzed by a focus on negative outcomes.

I had allowed myself to fall back into a defeated mindset. I simply had to refocus myself on my new mindset and imagine even more powerful scenarios of me succeeding. I needed to feel such joy and pride in my triumph that all my self-talk spoke of success, overcoming, and conquering.

Refocusing and spending time imagining myself accomplishing my goals is a major way that I broke through resistance on my tough days and got back to taking step-by-step action. Step-by-step action is how I accomplished every major thing I've ever done in my life, and it is how you can live your biggest, boldest life, too!

Live B-I-G! Belief! Imagination! Go forth!

Chapter Sixteen

So, how do you do the impossible? You've read a lot about how I have done the impossible over the years. How do you do it? I have two ideas that I'd like to share with you that, I hope, will inspire you.

My first idea centers around the art of magic. Magic has given me immense joy since I found it at age sixteen. I've met some of the most incredible people because of my study of magic. In fact, I've met most of my closest friends through magic.

I've traveled all over the world entertaining audiences because of magic. I have seen jaws drop wide open and bad moods instantly evaporate because of the power of wonder and amazement that comes from magic. Magic has been a real blessing in my life.

My first conscious efforts to do the impossible came with learning magic tricks. This may sound ridiculous, but every time I saw a new trick that amazed me, deep down I really hoped that I would learn some amazing secret that would open the secrets of the universe to me. And even though most of the time I only ended up learning about elastic bands, hidden threads, and adhesives, the lessons I learned about myself were definitely the best secrets.

If you recall, I had a belief when I was a teenager that there was no way I could learn sleight-of-hand. I've heard many people tell me that they couldn't possibly learn magic for all sorts of different reasons — from lack of coordination, to lack of sensation in their hands and fingertips, to whatever else they can dream up.

If you are like I was, and you don't think you can learn magic, let's use this opportunity to overcome that limiting belief, redefine what you think you are capable of, and do the impossible. The next chapter has three great magic tricks that you are capable of doing. Finish reading this chapter, then pick one of those tricks, and decide to learn it.

If you run into trouble learning through my descriptions and written tutorials, I am also going to give you a weblink you can visit to see me perform each trick and teach it to you via video.

I can't recommend highly enough learning, at least, a few magic tricks as a way to spread laughter and smiles to everyone you meet. At the right time and in the right place, everyone loves a good magic trick. What you will find is that kids love the experience of magic and adults love feeling like a kid again, even if it's just for a few moments.

And someday you might show someone a magic trick at a moment in life that they need it most — at a time when an escape from the troubles and worries of the day provides a real blessing to them.

My second idea on how you can do the impossible in your life is to dream big, beautiful, exciting dreams and open your mind to those possibilities. Once you've started dreaming of the things you want for your life, go back and re-read that last chapter. I put all the secrets of how to accomplish those dreams there.

As I shared my story with you in each chapter of this book, I tried to include examples of my beliefs, how I used my imagination, and the steps I took to overcome the challenges and accomplish my lofty goals. In the chapter you read before this one, I made a point to lay out specific ways that I used my B-I-G formula. Now you can use it too.

Is there a challenge in your life that feels impossible to overcome? Do you have a dream that you want to live, but it scares you to death?

In a nutshell, the first step toward doing the impossible is to change your belief. Change what you are telling yourself. If you are telling yourself that you can't accomplish something, then you will find that you are absolutely correct. You'll never be able to accomplish it. However, if you change your beliefs and open your mind to the idea that you can accomplish anything, the world will shift towards your success.

The second step is to see yourself, vividly, taking the steps and overcoming any challenge you put your mind to. See it in your mind and feel it in your soul. And live with that new vision. Allow it to permeate the depths of who you are. See yourself in a new light and you are well over half-way to the goal.

Finally, take step-by-step action. I've found that I can freak myself out by overthinking things. If instead, I just take action every single day toward my target, I am constantly amazed how quickly I am able to accomplish dreams and goals that felt impossible a short time before.

The real question here isn't how to do the impossible. You know how to do that now. The real question that I want to know the answer to is…What is possible?

I really do hope you will identify the first impossible challenge you are going to overcome. You'll be amazed how you view yourself in an exciting new light as you challenge yourself to live your dreams. So go ahead and ask yourself the question, "what will the first impossible challenge be that I overcome?" Find the answer, and enjoy a brand-new life of doing the impossible!

CHAPTER
SEVENTEEN

THE VERY FIRST card trick I learned was called "The Betting Card Trick" out of the book "Scarne on Card Tricks". I loved the idea that this was both a great trick and one that my spectators would want to place a wager on. To be honest, I wasn't even positive whether or not the trick would work, but when I performed it and saw my helper's reaction I knew I had a winner on my hands. I hope you will learn it and give it a try.

The Betting Card Trick

Effect: The performer gives the deck of cards a legitimate shuffle, fans them out, and then asks his helper to select one and remember it. He starts to cut small packets of cards from the top of the deck onto the table as he asks his helper to tell him to stop before he runs out of cards. When the helper says stop, the selected card is placed on top of the pile of cards on the table and then the remainder of the cards (that the performer is still holding) is placed on top of all the cards laying on the table. The cards are squared up so that everything is nice and neat.

The performer picks up the cards and holds them <u>face down</u> in his hand as he states that he is going to turn over cards one at a time and try to find the spectator's card. One at a time, he starts to turn cards <u>face up</u> onto the table so that everyone can see the value of each card he turns over.

After dealing many cards face up onto the table, the performer stops dealing, takes the next card off the top of the deck, and holds it face down in his hand, "I'll bet you that the next card I turn over will be your card." The helper can see that his card has already been dealt face up onto the table and that the performer is holding another card face down in his hand.

Obviously, the performer must be holding the wrong card face down in his hand, so the helper takes the bet. The performer wins the bet when he places the card in his hand back down on the top of the deck, reaches into the cards that have already been dealt face up to the table, and turns the helper's selected card over – face down.

Method: The method of finding the helper's card is simple. The real key to this trick is in the presentation.

At some point before the helper replaces his selected card you must glimpse the bottom card of the deck. There are many times that you can do this. I'll outline a few possibilities.

Possibility #1 - You could remove the deck from the box and take a peek at the bottom card. Then, when you shuffle the cards just make sure that the bottom card of the deck always falls first in the shuffle and stays on bottom. This is very disarming since you are shuffling the cards. No one will suspect that you are controlling the card on the bottom of the deck.

Possibility #2 – When your helper selects a card, tell them to "burn that card into your memory." That should impress upon them the importance of remembering the card. They will take a moment to look at the card. Take a peek at the bottom of the deck at that time.

The best use of this possibility is for when you are performing for several people at once. The moment that your helper selects a card tell them to, "show the card to everyone." There will be several seconds during which your helper will be preoccupied making sure that everyone sees the card. No one will be paying attention to you as you glimpse the bottom card of the deck.

Possibility #3 (My preferred method) – Perform a very basic sleight-of-hand technique called an All-Around Square Up. This is a method for squaring the cards that allows you to get a glimpse of the bottom card of the deck in a very nonchalant fashion. Do an online search for it, or drop by my website (http://www.cardsharklifestyle.com) for an online tutorial.

Once you know the bottom card of the deck, you are almost home-free. By the way, this technique is called a "key card" principle because the "key card" that you already know is going to help you find the helper's card.

Begin to cut small packets of cards from the top of the deck onto the table placing each small packet of cards on top of each other and ask your helper to tell you to stop before you run out of cards. It's important to tell them to stop you before you run out of cards so that your key card doesn't get dropped onto the deck if you run out of cards. Don't worry. If you tell them to stop you before you run out, they will stop you before you run out of cards.

As soon as they stop you from cutting the cards onto the table, your helper places his card face down on the top of the face down cards that are now on the table. Once your helper places his card on to the cards on the table, then you place the rest of the cards that you are holding (with your key card on the bottom of those cards) on top of the entire stack. In other words, your key card gets placed right on top of your helper's selected card as the deck is reassembled.

Make sure the cards are nice and neat as you pick them up from the table. Mention that you will try to find his card as you start turning cards face up one at a time from the top of the deck and placing them onto the table so everyone can see the value of each card turned over.

When you turn over and see your key card, the very next card that you turn over will be your helper's card. You could immediately identify his card, but a better presentation is to continue dealing two or three cards past your helper's card then stop and take a card into your hand face down.

Now think about what your helper is seeing. He has just seen you deal a bunch of cards face up onto the table, one at a time, including his own card. He can see his card laying on the table with two or three cards laying on top of it. Now you have another, obviously incorrect card at your fingertips.

And then you say, "I'll bet you that the next card I turn over is your card."

Your helper assumes that you are referring to the card that you have at your fingertips. Of course he is going to accept the bet. It looks like a sure-thing.

You very calmly then place the card that you are holding back on top of the deck (still face down) and reach into the cards laying on the table and turn your helper's card over, fulfilling your claim and blowing your helper's mind!

For such a simple secret, the reaction that you will get from your helper, and anyone else watching, will thrill you.

My only other tip is to make sure that you say "…the next card I turn over is your card," or "…the next card I turn over will be your card." Your helper thinks you are saying that you are going to turn over the card in your hand and that it is going to be his. However, the actual words never claim that you are going to turn over the card you are holding. You only claim that **the next card** that you turn over will be his. Then you reach into the pile and turn his over.

To see a performance of this trick, visit my website – http://www.cardsharklifestyle.com

Setup: A deck of cards

Voodoo Ashes

Effect: The performer asks his helper to hold out her hands and close them into fists. He then asks her if she is left- or right-handed. When she answers that she is right-handed, he decides to continue the demonstration with her closed right hand.

The performer picks up a piece of paper and draws an outline of a right hand on it. As he is drawing he asks his helper if she has ever heard of something called "sympathetic magic." When she says no, he then asks if she has ever heard of voodoo. She answers that she has and the performer quickly says, "Don't worry, we're not going to do any voodoo. Voodoo is the best example of sympathetic magic. People who believe in voodoo believe that if you do something to a voodoo doll, like poke the doll in the arm with a pin, that somehow that action to the doll will manifest itself on the person that the doll represents." His helper nods. "That is sympathetic magic," he says.

The performer then takes out a lighter and scorches the paper in the middle of the hand that he has drawn. When he takes the lighter away from the paper there is a burn mark right in the middle of the palm. He then waves the paper over and under the closed fist of the spectator, not touching her in any way, and then asks her to open her hand and look inside her palm. There are dark ashes on the inside of her palm!

Method: In this excellent (and very strong) magic trick, the secret work occurs a long time before anyone ever knows. In fact, the secret move happens at a time when most people don't even realize the trick has begun. The real secret to the success of this routine is in how well you sell it. If you take your time and really sell the script, everyone is going to think you've got some crazy magic powers.

The secret is that you have some "ash" on your left middle finger and you touch your helper's palm and transfer the ash when you adjust her hands. Here is the script and choreography of the moves.

Before you begin the trick, get some "ash" on the pad of your left middle finger. The "ash" can be actual ash from a dirty ash tray, or it can be a very dark shade of eyeliner that you buy at any store and leave in your pocket for times when you want to perform this trick.

If you find yourself somewhere that has an ashtray full of ashes, just pick up the ashtray and place it somewhere else as you dip your middle finger into the middle of the ashes and get some of it stuck to your finger.

If you decide to use the eyeliner method, just put your hand in your pocket where the eyeliner is and rub some of the eyeliner onto the first pad of your middle finger. Don't make a big deal about this. This is supposed to happen long before anyone realizes that you are going to do a trick. There should be no attention on you when you do this.

Turn to your helper and tell her you would like to show her something that she will never forget. Ask her to hold out her hands. You should illustrate what you want her to do with your own hands. So, when you ask her to hold out her hands you also hold out your hands about waist high, palms down. Don't worry about the ashes on your fingertip. Because your hands are palm down no one should be able to see underneath your hands.

As soon as she mirrors your actions with her own hands, grasp her hands with your fingers underneath and your thumbs on top and lift (or lower) her hands about two inches as you say, "Right about there."

The moment that you grasp her hands, both of your middle fingers should contact both of her palms. Because you have "ash" on your left middle finger some of it will transfer to her right palm, which is facing the floor. If you think it is necessary, you can slightly smudge the ash into her palm as you adjust her hands to the spot you want them to be.

You immediately tell her to close both of her hands into fists. Once she does, you are home-free.

The only other thing you need to do is help her select her right hand. Since most people are right-handed, that is quite easy to do.

Ask her if she is right- or left-handed. If she says that she is right-handed reply, "Ok, we'll use your right hand. Put your left hand away."

If she says that she is left-handed, you simply say, "Ok, you're left handed? I need to use your non-dominant hand for this. So put away your left hand."

Ultimately, it doesn't matter what she says; you will adjust what you say to get the outcome you want.

Once she has her right hand ashed and closed in front of her, you can enjoy selling the presentation and the response that you get when you reveal the ashes inside her palm.

To see a performance of this trick, visit my website – http://www.cardsharklifestyle.com

Setup: A piece of paper, pen, lighter or matches, some "ashes" from a dirty ash tray or dark eyeliner.

The Appearing & Vanishing Handkerchief

Effect: The performer displays his very empty hands. He then mimes reaching into the air with his right hand, grabbing what appears to be nothing, and placing it into his left hand which forms into a loose fist. The last time that he mimes placing nothing into his fist he then immediately starts to remove a vibrant red silk streamer.

He shakes the streamer back and forth once or twice and then uses both empty hands to display both sides of it. He then holds the streamer in his right hand again as he forms a loose fist with his left hand again. He tucks the streamer back into his left fist and then opens both hands to show they are completely empty and the streamer has vanished into thin air.

Method: The method of this outstanding magic trick uses a magic tool called a "thumb tip." A thumb tip is a small hollow piece of plastic that is molded to look like and fit on your thumb. Because it is hollow, you can place a small object (like a silk streamer) inside of it and can still wear it on your thumb.

The thumb tip is one of the most versatile tools in a magician's arsenal. Over the years, magicians have created hundreds of tricks that use the thumb tip. This just happens to be one of the many. When handled properly, the camouflage of a thumb tip is so strong that you shouldn't have any reservations about using one.

I almost didn't include this trick in this chapter because you must purchase a thumb tip to perform this one. But then I thought about the first time I walked into a magic shop and the magician behind the counter absolutely blew my mind with this trick.

Do a search online for "magician's thumb tip" and you will find plenty of places that you can purchase one for just a couple of bucks. You will also need to purchase a small silk streamer. You should be able to get that from the same place you get the thumb tip. Or you could just visit my website (http://www.cardsharklifestyle.com) and get them directly from me.

To perform this routine, you need to secretly get the thumb tip, with the streamer inside, on your thumb. You can do this by having the thumb tip inside your pocket and putting your hand in your pocket and putting the thumb tip on your thumb.

When you start miming and grabbing nothing from the air, make sure that your thumb, with the thumb tip on it, is always pointing directly at your spectator. In other words, do not let the spectator see it from the side. The thumb tip will always be longer than your real thumb is and seeing your thumb with the thumb tip on it from the side will expose the method.

The last time that you mime placing nothing into your other hand, drop off the thumb tip in that hand as you close your hand loosely in a fist. You will then be able to immediately reach into your loose fist with your free hand and start pulling out the silk streamer.

As soon as the streamer comes completely out of the thumb tip, put the thumb tip back on your thumb and you will be able to display your hands empty except for the streamer you are holding. Just remember to make sure that your thumb points directly at your spectator to mask the extra length of the tip.

To make the streamer vanish, reverse your actions. Place the thumb tip back in your left hand, then stuff the streamer inside of your loose fist (actually inside of the thumb tip inside your loose fist), then pretend to push the streamer tight into your fist with each of your fingers and steal the thumb tip out of your fist as your thumb "packs it tight" the final time. Slowly open your fist to show the silk streamer has vanished.

Setup: Silk streamer or silk handkerchief inside thumb tip which is inside your pocket.

A set up for one of my card shark shows.   Photo by Adam Sain

As we wrap up, I wanted to share a couple of thoughts with you about performing magic for the public.

When you perform magic for the public, you are going to have people ask you to tell them how you do your tricks. Sometimes they are going to almost beg you to tell them. At some point, you are going to genuinely consider telling your audience how you did the trick(s).

Listen carefully to me. I am speaking from experience here. Do not tell them how the trick is accomplished. I've made this mistake before and I'll tell you right now what is going to happen if you also make it.

The moment you decide to tell your helper how the magic trick works, you are going to see the wonder and amazement that is in their eyes turn to disappointment as they realize that your secret isn't that amazing.

The truth is that the secrets to most magic tricks are a little disappointing once you know them. The experience of magic is far more fun and amazing. When the secrets are unknown, your helpers dream of incredible possibilities. When your spectators know how simple the secrets are, the experience of magic will vanish and they may even feel foolish for being tricked.

That doesn't mean the secrets are not important. They are incredibly important. You just don't want your helpers to lose the experience of magic because they focus on the secrets. Magic occurs in your spectator's mind. Honor that magic and allow your helpers to enjoy it by not spoiling the fun.

If you've read these magic tricks and the idea of performing them excites you, then give them a try. These are three fantastic magic tricks that I learned at the very beginning of my journey learning magic. In the right place and at the right time, I still use them. That's how good they are.

Now before you go out and start performing these tricks I want you to promise me that you will practice them enough so that you can perform them successfully when you decide to do them. The biggest reason most people fail at magic is because they didn't practice enough by themselves before they decided to show someone their new trick. Take the time to learn the tricks fully and then take the time to rehearse them so you are successful when you perform them.

And if, by chance, you happen to mess up or get busted on a trick, don't worry about it. Screwing up a magic trick isn't the end of the world. Every magic trick takes a little bit of performance time before you have all the bugs worked out of it.

If you would like to learn more magic tricks, drop by my website anytime (www.cardsharklifestyle.com) and learn the latest tricks, cool moves, and much more.

Good luck!

ABOUT THE AUTHOR

Jason Michaels is a professional speaker and entertainer with astounding expertise in the arts of deception. A storyteller by heart, Jason loves to blend impossible mysteries with unforgettable tales. He has been performing sleight-of-hand, the art of illusion, and theater for over twenty-five years.

SPEAKER:

Diagnosed with Tourette's Syndrome at age six, Jason has overcome "the impossible" and become an internationally award-winning sleight-of-hand artist and professional speaker. He motivates audiences to see beyond their challenges and self-imposed limitations and inspires them to take action by living bigger, bolder lives with his keynote program "You Can Do the Impossible, Too!"

ENTERTAINER:

Jason has shared his style of interactive sleight-of-hand, illusion, and humor with corporate audiences, theaters, universities, the United States Armed Forces, and for private social affairs all over the world.

Urgent Plea!

Thank you for reading my book! I really

appreciate your feedback, and I love

hearing what you have to say.

I need your input to make future versions better.

Please leave me a helpful REVIEW on Amazon here -

https://www.amazon.com/dp/099892900X/

Thanks so much!!

~Jason

SELF-PUBLISHING

SCHOOL

NOW IT'S YOUR TURN

Discover the EXACT 3-step blueprint you need to become a bestselling author in 3 months.

Self-Publishing School helped me, and now I want them to help you with this FREE VIDEO SERIES!

Even if you're busy, bad at writing, or don't know where to start, you CAN write a best-seller and build your best life.

With tools and experience across a variety of niches and professions,Self-Publishing School is the only resource you need to take your book to the finish line!

DON'T WAIT

Watch this FREE VIDEO SERIES now, and Say "YES" to becoming a bestseller.

Go here: https://xe172.isrefer.com/go/ sps4fta-vts/bookbrosinc2451

RESOURCES/ INDEX

Jason Michaels (Speaker and Entertainer)
jasonmichaelsmagic.com

CardShark LifeStyle (basic magic tutorials and to purchase
magic tricks)
www.cardsharklifestyle.com

Tourette's Syndrome Association of America
www.tourette.org

International Brotherhood of Magicians
www.magician.org

Society of American Magicians
www.magicsam.com

Made in the USA
Columbia, SC
08 February 2021